The SYBEX

CW00573481

WORDSTAR
INSTANT
REFERENCE

The SYBEX Prompter Series

We've designed the SYBEX Prompter Series to meet the evolving needs of software users, who want essential information presented in an accessible format. Our best authors have distilled their expertise into compact *Instant Reference* books you can use to look up the precise use of any command—its syntax, available options, and operation. More than just summaries, these books also provide realistic examples and insights into effective usage drawn from our authors' wealth of experience.

The SYBEX Prompter Series also includes these titles:

The SYBEX Prompter™ Series

WORDSTAR®
INSTANT
REFERENCE

David J. Clark

San Francisco • Paris • Düsseldorf • London

The SYBEX Prompter Series
Editor in Chief: Rudolph S. Langer
Managing Editor: Barbara Gordon
Series Editor: James A. Compton
Editor: Alan Hislop

Cover design by Thomas Ingalls + Associates
Series design by Ingrid Owen
Screen reproductions produced by XenoFont

dBASE is a trademark of Ashton-Tate.
GEM is a trademark of Digital Research, Inc.
Laser Jet Series II is a registered trademark of Hewlett-Packard Corporation.
Mace Utilities is a trademark of Paul Mace Software.
MailList, TelMerge, and WordStar are trademarks of MicroPro International.
1-2-3 and Symphony are trademarks of Lotus Development Corporation.
OS/2, Presentation Manager, and Windows are trademarks of Microsoft Corporation.
Macintosh is a trademark of Apple Computer Corporation.
Quattro is a trademark of Borland International.
The Norton Utilities is a trademark of Peter Norton Computing.
Word Finder is a trademark of Microlytics, Inc.
XenoFont is a trademark of XenoSoft.

SYBEX is a registered trademark and Prompter Series is a trademark of SYBEX Inc.

SYBEX is not affiliated with any manufacturer.

Every effort has been made to supply complete and accurate information. However, SYBEX assumes no responsibility for its use, nor for any infringements of patents or other rights of third parties which would result.

Library of Congress Card Number: **88-62083**
ISBN **0-89588-543-3**
Printed by Haddon Craftsmen
Manufactured in the United States of America
10 9 8 7 6 5 4 3 2 1

To my parents

ACKNOWLEDGMENTS

I owe a debt of gratitude to all the people on the SYBEX staff who bore with me while I was writing this book and guided the manuscript on its arduous route to publication. I would like to thank Dianne King, Acquisitions Editor, Dr. R. S. Langer, Editor in Chief, and Barbara Gordon, Managing Editor, for allowing me the opportunity to write this book; Jim Compton, Prompter Series Editor, for useful insight throughout the project; Alan Hislop, Copyeditor, for his attentive editing; Joel Kroman, Technical Editor, for his meticulous attention to detail and quality; Bob Myren and Scott Campbell for their timely and efficient word processing (using WordStar); Sylvia Townsend, Proofreader, for her careful review; Charles Cowens, Typesetter, for his cooperation and patience; and Sonja Schenk, Graphics Technician, for screen production.

I would also like to thank Cheryl Hanley and David Cannon at MicroPro International for their cooperation and help during the pre-release stages of WordStar Professional Release 5.

TABLE OF CONTENTS

INTRODUCTION

How to Use This Book

This book has been designed and written to give you the most information in the least amount of time about any feature of WordStar Professional, Releases 4 and 5 for computers using the MS-/PC-DOS operating system. To take full advantage of this Instant Reference, read these few paragraphs first to see how the material has been organized.

If you are just learning to use WordStar, Part I, "The Word-Star Menus," gives an introductory tour of WordStar's features and the categories of commands into which these features are divided—called *menus.* This section also provides experienced users with a quick view of the changes in Release 5 of Word-Star. (The sample screens printed in this book show the Release 5 versions of these menus, except where noted.)

Part II, "Topical Reference," is an alphabetically arranged set of discussions on topics most often encountered in using WordStar. Think of this section as your "desk encyclopedia" of word processing. Cross-referenced like an index, it allows you to look up any task you want to learn how to perform, any feature you want to learn how to use, without knowing the exact expression WordStar uses to describe it. For example, if you want to know how to look up synonyms while editing onscreen, you will be directed to the information whether you look up Synonyms, Thesaurus, or Word Finder (the name WordStar gives to this feature in Release 4). You can also find entries for concepts unique to WordStar that need more explanation, such as dot commands or the ruler line.

For each operation or feature you'll find the following information:

- the WordStar release (4, 5, or both) in which the feature is available

- a key sequence showing at a glance the exact keystrokes or menu selections to use in carrying out the operation in each of its variant forms

- a usage discussion explaining how the key sequence works, noting any rules or restrictions that apply to the feature and offering valuable tips on using it effectively

- a list of any related entries you can consult for further information

Broader topics are divided into sections on individual operations; these sections also contain the items listed above.

To help you quickly find the information you need, main entry names appear in the page headers; section titles within these entries (such as "Conditional Merge Commands" within **Merge Print**) are listed in the Table of Contents.

Finally, Appendix A shows how to install WordStar and discusses ways of tailoring it to your specific needs and preferences.

Take a few minutes to leaf through these pages and get acquainted with the format—you'll soon see that this little book can save you lots of time and effort.

Conventions Used in This Book

The following conventions have been used throughout the book. In Part II, when you see the term *Classic menu*, it refers to both the menu system of Release 4 and the menu system of Release 5 set to help level 3 or below; the term *pull-down menu* refers to the menu system available with help level 4 of Release 5. (Help levels are discussed in Part I under the heading "Setting Your Help Level" and in Part II under **Help**.) The table below shows some other conventions.

EXAMPLE	EXPLANATION
[from the Opening menu]	Square brackets enclose comments (not keystrokes to be typed in) *or*
[px]	Keystrokes that may be typed to use optional features of a given command—don't type the square brackets.
<text string>	A value to be specified by the user—don't type the angle brackets.
↵	This symbol represents the Enter or Return key on your keyboard.
^C	WordStar uses the caret (^) character to symbolize the Ctrl ("control") key on your keyboard, used to initiate most commands in Release 4 and the Classic menus in Release 5. This example means "hold down the **Ctrl** key and then press **C**."
Shift-F1	This means "hold down the **Shift** key and press **F1**."
EDIT/File/Print a file...	The slash symbol (/) is used in this book to separate stages in a sequence of menu selections. This example means "select **Print a file...** from the File pull-down menu on the EDIT menu bar."

PART I

The WordStar User Interface

Over the course of a decade, MicroPro has developed, adapted, and improved WordStar's *user interface* to take into account the changing preferences and increasing capabilities of WordStar's audience. (The interface is the set of commands, menus, and instructions that enables the user to interact with the program.) The interface has five parts: the pull-down menu system (new to Release 5), the Classic menu system (the traditional menu system including control commands), the editing screen, the dot commands, and the function keys. Following is a brief explanation of each part.

The WordStar Pull-Down Menus (Release 5 Only)

The WordStar pull-down menus have been designed to incorporate IBM's Systems Applications Architecture (SAA), a set of conventions that attempts to standardize the behavior, format, and appearance of programs that run on IBM PCs. This new menu system differs from the earlier system, referred to by MicroPro as the Classic menu system. If you have a copy of WordStar prior to Release 5, move on to the section entitled "The WordStar Classic Menus."

Because experienced WordStar users are used to the earlier system, the new pull-down menu system has been designed as an alternative, not a replacement; not all WordStar commands are available from pull-down menus. The advantage of the pull-down menus is that they are easy to use. Beginners can get started in WordStar much more quickly and comfortably than was previously possible. Intermediate and advanced WordStar users can also benefit from the pull-down menus when they use less familiar features or many of the features new to Release 5. The alternative Classic commands are listed to the right of the command descriptions on the pull-down menus, so that if you use an option frequently, you can learn the quicker Classic command for invoking the feature.

The pull-down menus are so named because they are activated by pressing a letter on the menu bar that displays a menu of options directly underneath it. This is much like the mouse-driven menu systems found on the Apple Macintosh as well as on GEM, Microsoft Windows, and OS/2 Presentation Manager, which require that the user pull down the menu by clicking and then dragging with a mouse device. A mouse is not needed to operate WordStar, and mouse capability is not incorporated in the program. However, through the use of the cursor keypad and standard WordStar cursor commands, the pull-down menu system functions in a similar fashion. Following is a brief description of the pull-down menus and how they work.

The Opening Screen

In Release 5 of WordStar Professional, the first screen you see is the Opening screen, shown in Figure 1.1. Across the top of the screen appears a menu bar with the names of three menus with the first letter highlighted. From this menu bar, you can access all other menus and commands in WordStar. Three commands are possible from this menu bar:

F   Opens the File menu, where most of the editing, file management, and printing operations and commands are located.

O   Opens the Other menu, which contains commands for generating lists, running DOS commands, changing the help level, displaying the RAM (Random Access Memory) usage of your computer, and shorthand macros (keystroke-saving commands).

A   Takes you to the Additional menu, which contains MailList and TelMerge, programs that generate documents from mailing lists and perform telecommunications, respectively.

Below the menu bar is a list of all the files in your current directory, along with their size in kilobytes. You can also press F1 to access WordStar's help feature, which, if pressed at this point, will display information about the Opening menu.

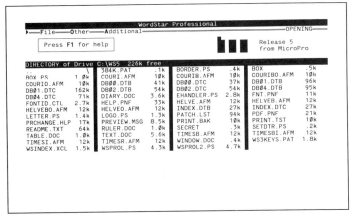

WordStar Professional

►——File——Other——Additional——————————————OPENING——

Press **F1** for help   Release 5
                                         from MicroPro

DIRECTORY of Drive C:\WS5 226k free

. .	\	384K.PAT	.1k	BORDER.PS	.4k	BOX	.5k
BOX.PS	1.Øk	COURI.AFM	1Øk	COURIB.AFM	1Øk	COURIBO.AFM	1Øk
COURIO.AFM	1Øk	DBØØ.DTB	41k	DBØØ.DTC	37k	DBØ1.DTB	96k
DBØ1.DTC	162k	DBØ2.DTB	54k	DBØ2.DTC	54k	DBØ4.DTB	95k
DBØ4.DTC	71k	DIARY.DOC	3.6k	EHANDLER.PS	2.8k	FNT.PNF	11k
FONTID.CTL	2.7k	HELP.PNF	33k	HELVE.AFM	12k	HELVEB.AFM	12k
HELVEBO.AFM	12k	HELVEO.AFM	12k	INDEX.DTB	27k	INDEX.DTC	27k
LETTER.PS	1.4k	LOGO.PS	1.3k	PATCH.LST	94k	PDF.PNF	21k
PRCHANGE.HLP	17k	PREVIEW.MSG	8.5k	PRINT.BAK	1Øk	PRINT.TST	1Øk
README.TXT	64k	RULER.DOC	1.Øk	SECRET	.3k	SETDTR.PS	.2k
TABLE.DOC	1.Øk	TEXT.DOC	5.6k	TIMESB.AFM	12k	TIMESBI.AFM	12k
TIMESI.AFM	12k	TIMESR.AFM	12k	WINDOW.DOC	.4k	WS3KEYS.PAT	1.8k
WSINDEX.XCL	1.5k	WSPROL.PS	4.3k	WSPROL2.PS	4.7k		

Figure 1.1: The Opening screen, WordStar Release 5

You can bypass the Opening screen and perform a Word-Star operation immediately by typing one of the following commands from the DOS prompt. (If you have Release 4, use a space instead of a slash (/) to separate the file name from the option letter.)

WS *<filename.ext>*   Opens a file in document mode.

WS *<filename.ext>* **/d**   Opens a file in document mode when WordStar has been set to nondocument mode in WSCHANGE.

WS *<filename.ext>* **/m**   Merge prints a file and returns to the Opening menu (Release 5 only).

WS *<filename.ext>* **/n**   Opens a file in nondocument mode.

WS *<filename.ext>* **/p**   Prints a file and returns to the Opening menu.

WS /s   Opens a Speed Write file (Release 5 only).

WS *<filename.ext>* / *<o>* /**x**   Used following another
option letter *<o>* to exit
WordStar once that opera-
tion has been completed.
In Release 4, there can be
no spaces between the
first option and **x**.

WS *<filename.ext>* /**[n**   Executes a shorthand
macro using the File menu
(the file name specifica-
tion is optional). If a file
name is specified, this
command performs the
operation selected on that
file.

For more information on bypassing the Opening screen, see
Starting WordStar in the Topical Reference Section.

The File Menu   The File menu, shown in Figure 1.2, is
reached by pressing **F** from the Opening screen. The option
at the top of the list (Speed Write in this case) is always highlighted in any pull-down menu. If you want to select the first
option, you can press ↵. To select another option, you can use
the cursor movement keys (either the WordStar cursor codes
or the directional arrows on the numeric keypad) to move the
highlighting bar to the desired option and then press ↵, or
you can press the letter or combination of letters listed to the
right of the selection. You can use either upper- or lowercase
letters here; WordStar does not distinguish between them
when typed as commands. If the letter or letters appear dim,
this means they can only be selected using the cursor movement keys.

The File menu offers you 11 options. Table 1.1 lists these
options and the keystrokes necessary to invoke them.

For more information on these commands, see the relevant
entries in the Topical Reference section.

KEYSTROKE	OPTION	DESCRIPTION
S	Speed Write (new file)	Opens a new file.
D	Open a document file	Opens an existing document file.
N	Open a non-document file	Opens a nondocument (command or programming) file.
P	Print a file	Prints a file.
M	Merge print a file	Inserts (merges) data to an existing file to produce a new printed file.
L	Change drive/directory	Changes the current drive and/or directory without leaving WordStar.
O	Copy a file	Makes a copy of an existing file, allowing you to assign a new name to the file and/or copy it to a different drive or directory.
Y	Delete a file	Deletes any file(s) designated unless they are protected; DOS wildcard commands can be used to delete groups of files.
E	Rename a file	Renames a file.
C	Protect/un-protect a file	Protects file from alteration or deletion, or removes this protection.
X	Exit WordStar	Exits WordStar and returns to DOS.

Table 1.1: The File menu options, WordStar Release 5

The Other Menu   The Other menu (Figure 1.3) is accessed by pressing **O** from the Opening menu. The supplemental WordStar commands it contains are not directly involved with text editing.

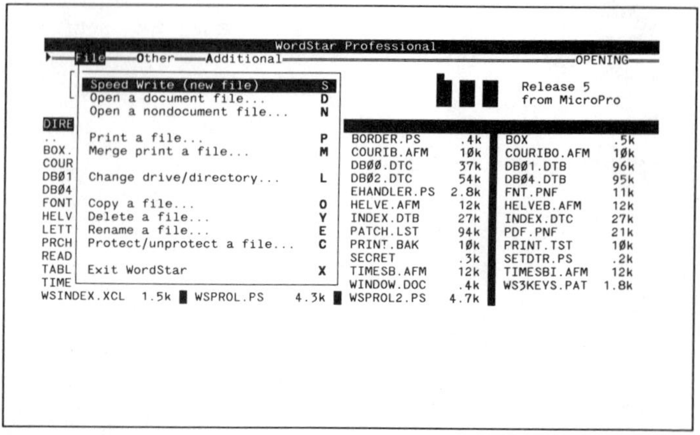

Figure 1.2: The File menu, WordStar Release 5

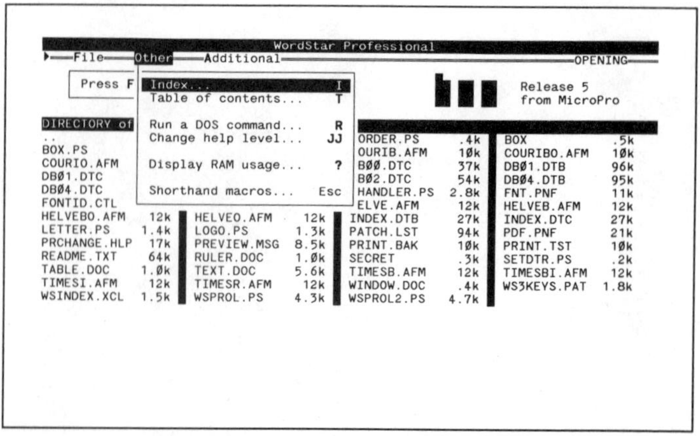

Figure 1.3: The Other menu, WordStar Release 5

For more information on the options available from the Other menu, see **Help**, **Index**, **RAM Usage**, **Run a DOS Command**, **Shorthand**, and **Table of Contents** in the Topical Reference section.

The Additional Menu   The Additional menu contains commands to access two auxiliary programs, MailList (a program for generating mailing lists) and TelMerge (a communications program). To reach this menu, shown in Figure 1.4, press **A** from the Opening menu. For more information on MailList and TelMerge, see their respective entries in the Topical Reference section.

The Edit Screen

Once you have selected either Speed Write to open a new document or Open a Document File from the File menu, the screen shown in Figure 1.5 appears. A menu bar runs across the second horizontal line on the screen (it does not appear in Release 4). This line shows the various pull-down menus available while editing a file.

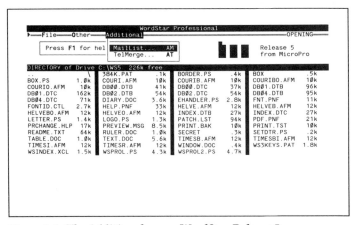

Figure 1.4: The Additional menu, WordStar Release 5

While editing a document, you can access pull-down menus either by pressing the Alt key in combination with the first letter of the menu you want to pull down, by pressing **Alt-Spacebar** and then the first letter of the menu, or by pressing **Alt-Spacebar** and then moving to the desired pull-down menu with the cursor movement keys. Thus, to pull down the EDIT/File menu, for example, you can either press **Alt-F**, **Alt-Spacebar F**, **Alt-Spacebar ^D**, or **Alt-Spacebar →**. Most WordStar commands are available from these menus. A brief description of each of these menus follows.

The EDIT/File Menu   To pull down the EDIT/File menu, press **Alt-F**. You will see the menu shown in Figure 1.6. As you can see from this figure, the EDIT/File menu on the editing screen allows you to perform file operations similar to those available from the Opening menu, but with a few important differences. Instead of allowing you to open documents, EDIT/File lets you either save a document and return to editing, save a document with a new name, save the document and go to the Opening screen, save the document and exit WordStar, or abandon any changes made and return to the Opening screen. It also allows you to print, merge print, copy, delete, or rename a document, as well as change the

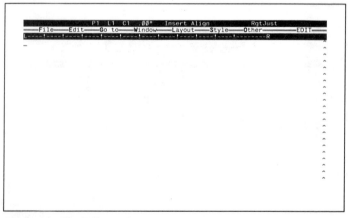

Figure 1.5: The Edit screen, WordStar Release 5

drive and/or directory, just as in the File menu from the Opening screen.

Note that to the right of each of these options is a key combination of two or three letters beginning with ^K. To activate any of these commands, you must press the Ctrl key at the same time you press K, and then press the second (and sometimes third) letter. Alternatively, you can move the highlight bar with the cursor movement keys until the desired option is selected and then press ⏎.

The EDIT/Edit Menu   As with the EDIT/File menu, you access the EDIT/Edit menu by pressing Alt with the first letter of the menu: **Alt-E**. Doing so produces the menu shown in Figure 1.7. From this pull-down menu you can undo a command, delete a word or line, or execute numerous operations on *blocks* of text. A block in WordStar is a section of marked text on which you perform operations as a unit. You can delete, move, copy, hide, or show a block, as well as mark a column as a block. You can insert an existing file into your current file as a block or copy a block to a new file. As with the EDIT/File menu, commands from the EDIT/Edit menu can be executed either by pressing Ctrl in combination with the appropriate

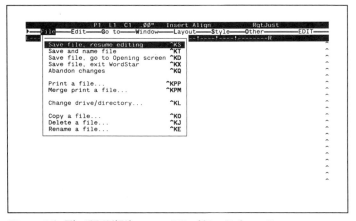

Figure 1.6: The EDIT/File menu, WordStar Release 5

letter(s) listed to the right of the option or by moving the highlight bar to the desired option and pressing ↵.

For more information on the commands on the EDIT/Edit menu, see **Block Operations**, **Delete**, **Merge Print, Spreadsheet,** and **Undo** in the Topical Reference section.

The EDIT/Go To Menu   To access the EDIT/Go To menu, press **Alt-G** from the Edit screen. The pull-down menu shown in Figure 1.8 will appear. For more information on the EDIT/Go To menu, see **Go To** and **Replace** in the Topical Reference section.

The EDIT/Window Menu   To pull down the EDIT/Window menu, press **Alt-W** from the Edit screen. The menu shown in Figure 1.9 appears. This menu contains commands to use windows, a feature new to Release 5 of WordStar. You can divide the Edit screen into two windows, switch between them, copy or move a block from one window to the other, or close windows from this menu. For more information on this new windowing feature of WordStar, see **Block Operations** and **Window** in the Topical Reference section.

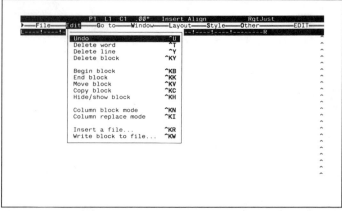

Figure 1.7: The EDIT/Edit menu, WordStar Release 5

The EDIT/Layout Menu The EDIT/Layout menu contains commands governing the arrangement of your text on
the page. To access this menu, press **Alt-L**. The screen will
look like Figure 1.10.

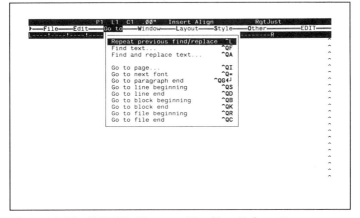

Figure 1.8: The EDIT/Go To menu, WordStar Release 5

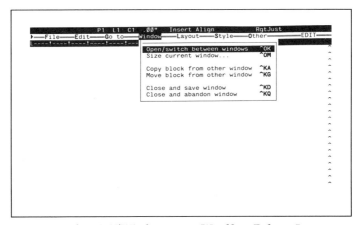

Figure 1.9: The EDIT/Window menu, WordStar Release 5

For more information about the commands on the EDIT/Layout menu, see **Align Paragraphs, Centering, Headers, Footers, Line Spacing, Margins, Page Breaks, Page Numbering, Page Preview, Paragraph Numbering, Right Justification,** and **Tabs** in the Topical Reference section.

The EDIT/Style Menu   The EDIT/Style menu contains commands that govern the appearance of type on the printed page. When you press **Alt-S**, the menu shown in Figure 1.11 appears. From this menu you can select boldfacing, underlining, italics, subscript, superscript, strikeout, and different fonts. Although almost all printers can produce boldface and underlined type, the number of other options that you can actually produce on paper depends on the capabilities of your printer.

When you use one of the commands from the Style menu, it will remain in effect in that document until you select it again to turn it off. You will see a code inserted into the text. For example, ^B appears at the beginning and end of a section of boldface text. Also, depending on your type of monitor, all text affected will appear boldfaced, underlined, or in a different color to distinguish it from normal text. If you find the codes distracting (which they can be, especially when you

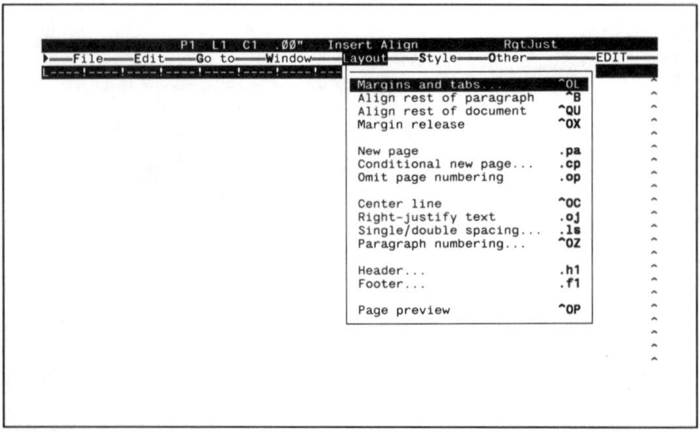

Figure 1.10: The EDIT/Layout menu, WordStar Release 5

are trying to align columns in tabular text), you can suppress them by selecting Hide/Display Controls; the codes
will disappear, but the boldface, underlining, or alternate
color will not.

For more information on the commands in the Style menu,
see **Boldface**, **Choose Font**, **Hide/Display Controls**, **Italics/
Color**, **Strikeout**, **Subscript**, **Superscript**, and **Underline** in
the Topical Reference section.

The EDIT/Other Menu   The EDIT/Other menu is a catch-
all menu that contains commands to access various ancillary
programs. To access the EDIT/Other menu, press **Alt-O**. The
menu shown in Figure 1.12 will appear. For more information
on the options offered by this menu, see **Block Operations**,
Calculator, **Help**, **Notes**, **Run a DOS Command**, **Spell**, and
Thesaurus in the Topical Reference section.

The WordStar Classic Menus

This section describes the WordStar Classic menu system. The
Classic menus appear on the screen when your help level is
set to 3 or when you pause while issuing a control command

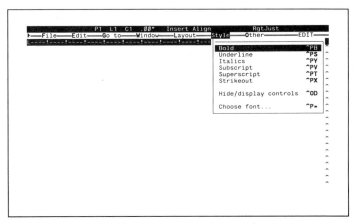

Figure 1.11: The EDIT/Style menu, WordStar Release 5

with your help level set to 2. The Classic Opening menu appears every time you start WordStar, unless you are using Release 5, help level 4. For more information on the help levels, read "Setting Your Help Level," which follows shortly.

In order to conserve space, some minor WordStar commands are not listed on the menus, but they can be invoked directly from the keyboard in the same manner as those displayed. All of the commands that don't appear on either the pull-down or Classic menus are listed and explained in the Topical Reference Section. Following is a description of each principal menu and the most frequently used commands it contains, along with some help in moving between menus.

The Opening Menu

The Opening menu (Figure 1.13) is the list of command options you see at the top of your screen when you first load WordStar. It is the main menu through which all other menus are eventually reached. The letters listed to the left of each command option invoke that command. Although these letters are uppercase, WordStar does not distinguish between

Figure 1.12: The EDIT/Other menu, WordStar Release 5

upper- and lowercase letters in commands; you can press either one.

Setting Your Help Level   The first question many people ask about any program is, "Where do I go for help?" In Word-Star, the first place to look is the help option on the Opening menu. Press **J** (help) and you will see a new screen filled with information about the Opening menu. WordStar's Help feature is *contextual*, that is, it provides information about whichever operation you're currently using.

You've probably found that you need less information to perform operations the more you use the program, and you may begin to find the menu displays distracting. For this reason, WordStar lets you set your own help level by adjusting the amount of information you are given. Press **J** once more to see the five possible levels of the Help feature, 0–4.

4   Release 5 only: all pull-down menus, prompts, confirmations ("Are you sure?") are on.

3   All Classic menus, prompts, confirmations, are on.

2   Edit menu is off; other menus are on.

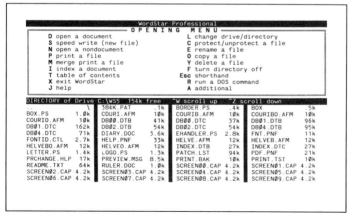

Figure 1.13: The Opening menu

1   All menus (except Opening), prompts, confirmations are off.

0   All menus (except Opening), prompts, the status line, and most confirmations are off. In Release 5 you can also copy, move, and delete hidden blocks.

In WordStar Release 4, only four settings, 0–3, are available, since there are no pull-down menus in that version.

For more information about the Help feature, see **Help** in the Topical Reference section.

Opening Files   From the Opening menu you can perform operations on the files in the current directory (listed below the menu) or create new files. In Release 5, you can open a new file by pressing **S** (speed write). To open a new file in Release 4, press **D** (open a document) and then type the file's name and then press ↵. To open an existing file in either release, press **D** and type the file's name and then press ↵, or press **D** (open a document) and then press **^X** (hold the Ctrl key down while pressing X) and the cursor will appear on the first file in the directory. Use the cursor keys to select the file you want to open and press ↵. Both methods take you to the Edit menu, discussed below. To open a file that you want to use as a command file, a data file for merge printing, or that you will use with another program, such as a programming language, database program, or another word processor, press **N** (open a nondocument) instead and follow the same procedures. For more information on these options, see **Document Mode** and **Nondocument Mode** in the Topical Reference section.

Printing   WordStar has two printing functions: printing a single file, and *merge printing*. Merge printing takes information from more than one file and merges it to create a single document or set of documents. To print a single file, press **P** (print a file) and select the file by typing its name or highlighting it in the directory in the same manner as mentioned above. To merge print a file, press **M** (merge print a file) and then select a file. For more information on printing operations, see **Merge Print** and **Print** in the Topical Reference section.

File Management Commands   These commands have functions similar to those your operating system (DOS) provides for certain housekeeping tasks such as renaming, copying, deleting, protecting, listing file directories, and moving between drives and directories. Performing these tasks from within Wordstar is often more convenient and sometimes safer because WordStar provides you with step-by-step instructions and Help messages along the way. To change a file's name, press **E** (rename a file); to copy a file, press **O** (copy a file); to delete a file, press **Y** (delete a file); to protect a file (from accidental deletion or alteration) press **C** (protect a file); to change your directory, press **L** (change logged drive/directory); and to turn the display of the current directory off or on, press **F** (turn directory off/on). To display the amount of memory in use by your computer, press **?**.

For more information on file management on the Opening menu, see **Copy**, **Delete**, **Drive**, **Protect/Unprotect**, **RAM Usage**, and **Rename** in the Topical Reference section.

Creating Lists   WordStar can compile two types of lists: an index, or a table of contents. The index takes all the words and phrases you have marked in a file and sorts them in alphabetical order, followed by the page number of each occurrence. To invoke this command, press **I** (index a document) and then select a file. The table of contents feature allows you to create up to ten lists of headings (or illustrations or notes) in the order in which they occur in your document, followed by the page number, if you want. To create a table of contents, press **T** (table of contents). For more information on creating lists, see **Index** and **Table of Contents** in the Topical Reference section.

Saving Keystrokes   As you work you may find a sequence of keystrokes, be it a set of commands or a standard phrase you type over and over, that you wish you could condense into one or two keystrokes. In computer programs, these condensed keystrokes are called *macros*. WordStar's macro feature is called the Shorthand menu. It is accessed by pressing **Esc** (shorthand). See the section "The Shorthand Menu" below for more details.

Leaving WordStar   Before you turn off your computer, it is necessary to exit from the WordStar program to the disk operating system (DOS). If you don't quit your work session in this fashion, you risk damaging your program files and losing your work. To exit properly from the Opening menu, press **X** (exit WordStar). If you want to run a DOS command (such as CHKDSK, which looks for and identifies faulty sectors on your disk) from your operating system without actually leaving WordStar, press **R** (run a DOS command). WordStar will prompt you to enter a DOS command. Type in the DOS command and press ↵ to execute it. When the command has finished executing, you will see the message

Press any key to return to WordStar.

For more information on leaving WordStar, see **Exit** or **Run a DOS Command** in the Topical Reference section.

The Edit Menu

The Edit menu is the menu displayed at the top of your screen during editing if you have your help level set to 3, as shown in Figure 1.14.

For more detailed information on the commands on this menu, see **Align Paragraphs**, **Block Operations**, **Cursor Movement**, **Delete**, **Go To**, **Help**, **Insert**, **Replace**, **Scroll**, **Shorthand**, **Tabs**, and **Undo** in the Topical Reference section.

The Nondocument Edit Menu

The Nondocument Edit menu (Figure 1.15) is nearly identical to the Edit menu for documents with the following exceptions: ^B switches the top bit (that is, converts document files to nondocument files), and ^O allows you to set the tab width (there are no other onscreen format commands in nondocument mode in Release 4), turn print controls off, switch to the other window, size the window, set tabs, and set the cursor speed. For more information, see **ASCII Conversion** and **Nondocument Mode** in the Topical Reference section.

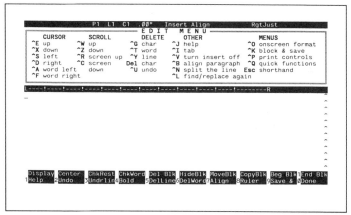

Figure 1.14: The Edit menu

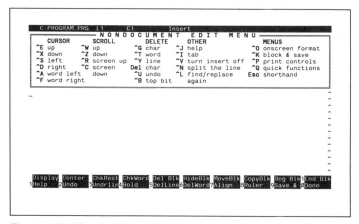

Figure 1.15: The Nondocument Edit menu

The Onscreen Format Menu

The Onscreen Format menu is activated by pressing ^O from the Edit screen. Commands on this menu govern aspects of the layout and format of your document that you can see on-screen before printing, as shown in Figure 1.16. From this menu you can set or release the margins, embed margin and tab settings into a document (using the ruler line), turn word wrap on and off, turn right justification on and off, enter soft hyphens (hyphens that print only at the end of a line), set and clear tabs, create temporary indents, set line spacing, and center text on a line. You can also suppress or display print control codes, dot commands, and soft spaces, and turn automated hyphen help on or off.

In Release 5, in addition to the features listed above, you can number paragraphs, turn the auto-align feature on and off (which automatically adjusts the alignment of text within margins as you edit), and preview what your document will look like when printed. You can open, switch between, or size windows, and you can access the Notes menu, shown in Figure 1.17.

For more information on items on the Onscreen Format menu, see **Auto-Align**, **Centering**, **Hide/Display Controls**,

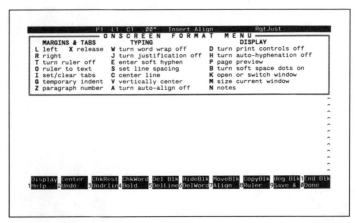

Figure 1.16: The Onscreen Format menu

Hyphenation, Indent, Index, Line Spacing, Margins, Notes, Page Preview, Right Justification, Ruler Line, Soft Space Display, Tabs, Window, and **Word Wrap** in the Topical Reference section.

The Block & Save Menu

The Block & Save menu (Figure 1.18) is activated by pressing **^K** from the Edit screen. The commands on this menu are divided into four categories: save commands, cursor commands, block commands, and file commands. You have several save options in WordStar. You can either save the file to disk and resume editing, save a file and return to the Opening menu, save and rename a file and return to the Opening menu (in Release 5 only), save a file and exit to DOS, or quit the file without saving it and return to the Opening menu. WordStar allows you to speed up cursor movement within a file from the Block & Save menu by placing up to ten place markers within a file and jumping quickly to any of these marked places by pressing any numeral between 0 and 9.

All of WordStar's block commands can be accessed through the Block & Save menu as well. You can mark a horizontal section of text or a vertical column of text, which WordStar refers

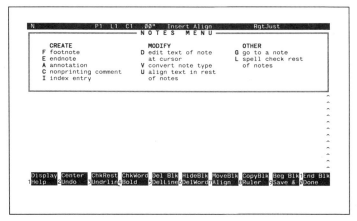

Figure 1.17: The Notes menu, WordStar Release 5

to as a *block*. Once marked, the block can be moved, copied, deleted, summed (if the block contains numbers), copied to a separate file on disk, or hidden. It can also be converted to all uppercase, lowercase, or (in Release 5) lowercase with upper-case letters at the beginnings of sentences. In Release 4, the case conversion commands are not displayed on the menu, al-though they function the same as the Block & Save commands.

The file commands available on the Block & Save menu allow you to perform file operations found on the Opening menu while you are still editing a file. In addition to the com-mands listed above, Release 5 allows you to keep your pre-vious edit and save your current file as a new file with a new name, copy or move a block between windows, perform a word count on a selected block, or sort text alphanumerically.

For more information on the commands contained in the Block & Save menu, see **Block Operations**, **Copy**, **Delete**, **Drive**, **Exit**, **Print**, **Run a DOS Command**, **Save**, **Sort**, **Win-dow**, and **Word Count** in the Topical Reference section.

The Quick Menu

The Quick menu is a catch-all menu of time-saving features that has increased in size with each updated version of Word-Star. It is shown in Figure 1.19.

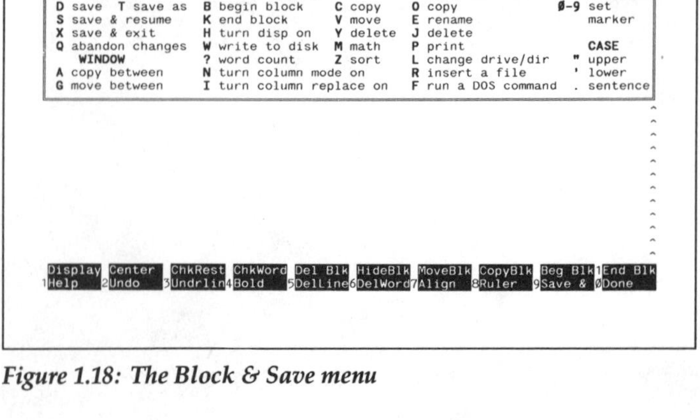

Figure 1.18: The Block & Save menu

New additions to the Quick menu for Release 5 are commands to allow you to go to the next font (**^Q=**) and go to the thesaurus (**^QJ**). Note that the thesaurus in Release 4 is a separate program that must be loaded into memory before starting WordStar and is reached by pressing **Alt-1**, which in Release 5 has an entirely different function: switching between the page preview and edit screens.

For more information on the various features included in the Quick menu, see **Align Paragraphs**, **Calculator**, **Character Count**, **Cursor Movement**, **Delete**, **Go To**, **Markers**, **Repeat**, **Replace**, **Spell**, **Scroll**, and **Thesaurus** in the Topical Reference section.

The Shorthand Menu

"Shorthand" is the term WordStar uses to describe the keystroke-saving feature usually referred to in computer parlance as the *macro* feature. This menu, shown in Figure 1.20, can be reached from either the Opening menu or the Edit menu by pressing **Esc**. The Shorthand feature allows you to program a combination of the Esc key and any letter or number (0–9) to represent a string of text and commands with just two keys. There are also preprogrammed commands to print the system

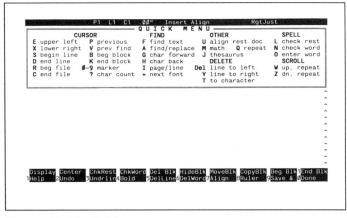

Figure 1.19: The Quick menu

date and time as text into your file and to print results from Block Math or the Calculator into your file in various formats. For more information on the Shorthand commands, see **Block Math**, **Calculator**, **Date**, **Shorthand**, and **Time** in the Topical Reference section.

The Print Controls Menu

The Print Controls menu (Figure 1.21) is reached by pressing **^P** from the Edit screen. Most of the commands on this menu control the appearance of your document when printed. The two leftmost columns of commands on the upper portion of this menu are labeled BEGIN & END because they are *toggle* commands; that is, you turn them on and off with the same command. For example, to turn bold on, you press **^PB**, and the rest of your document from that point forward will be boldface (and will appear brighter or in a different color on your screen) until you press **^PB** again to turn it off. Indexing, the last command in the two columns, does not affect the appearance of the printed document, but words are marked for indexing functions in much the same way as they are marked for print controls, and thus the command is included on this menu.

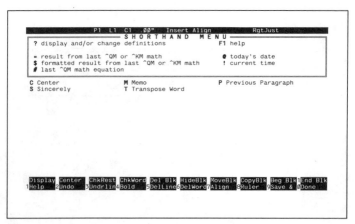

Figure 1.20: The Shorthand menu

The two rightmost columns of print control commands are not toggle commands; pressing them a second time doesn't turn them off. These commands usually issue a specialized command to the printer. For example, you can overprint a character with another character by pressing **^PH**, which allows you to add circumflexes, umlauts, cedillas, and so forth to foreign words. You can overprint a line by pressing **^P↵**, and you can select phantom space or rubout (these two characters are primarily for daisy-wheel printers that have more characters than exist on the keyboard) by pressing **^PF** or **^PG**, respectively. You can create up to four custom print controls (five in Release 5) by pressing **^P** in combination with **Q**, **W**, **E**, or **R** (or ! in Release 5)—a useful feature for selecting different fonts with a laser printer. For less complicated printing, you can switch between "normal" and "alternate" font (or pitch) by pressing **^PA** for alternate and **^PN** for normal. You can insert form feeds to have the printer advance to a new page without starting a new line by pressing **^PL**, or line feeds to have the printer advance to a new line by pressing **^PJ**.

Another print feature is the binding space, **^PO**, which allows you to keep two words together at the end of a line, even though they are separated by a space; this is useful with dates,

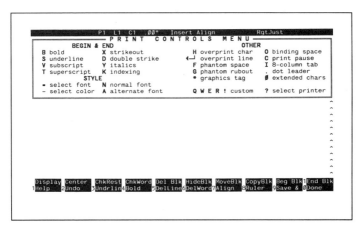

Figure 1.21: The Print Controls menu

names, and mathematical formulas. You can pause your printer in the middle of a file (to change printwheels or ribbon colors, for instance) by pressing **^PC**. You can insert a character to align text on the printed page as it does on the screen, even though you are using different pitches or proportional spacing, by pressing **^P@**. You can insert a fixed tab of eight spaces by pressing **^PI** when you want to show different levels in programming language routines.

Additional features that have been added to Release 5 include a separate command to select colors so that you can now use italics with a color printer, as well as use more than two colors, a graphics tag character to facilitate the insertion of graphic images in your document (to be used with a graphics program call Inset), a command to insert rows of dots between text (as in a table of contents), a command to insert extended ASCII characters into the text, and a command to select a new printer definition.

For more information on the various commands on this menu, see **Binding Space, Boldface, Choose Font, Column Alignment, Custom Print, Double Strike, Form Feed, Graphics Characters, Index, Italics, Italics/Color, Line Feed, Overprint, Phantom Rubout and Phantom Space, Pitch, Print, Print Pause, Strike Out, Subscript, Superscript,** and **Underline** in the Topical Reference section.

The Printing Menu

When you print or merge print a file in WordStar, whether from the Opening or the Edit menu, WordStar's default option allows you to perform other operations at the same time data is being sent to the printer. The print operation is indicated on the screen by the message

Printing

on the status line. If you want to interrupt or modify the printing operation in some way, you must press the same key combination you used to initiate the printing operation. When you do this, the Printing menu shown in Figure 1.22 appears on your screen.

From this menu you can temporarily halt the printing operation, abandon the operation, or resume printing after a pause. You also have the choice of whether to print at full speed, in which case no operations other than printing are possible, and WordStar devotes all its processing time to sending data to the printer, or to print in the background (the default option), in which case the Printing menu disappears, and you are allowed to perform any other operations you want except to exit from WordStar. For more information on this menu, see **Merge Print**, **Print**, and **Print Pause** in the Topical Reference section.

The Math Menu

To access WordStar's built-in calculator, press **M** from the Quick menu (**^QM** from the Edit menu). The Math menu shown in Figure 1.23 appears on your screen. The calculator allows you to perform basic arithmetic and trigonometric operations from within WordStar. Simply type an equation and press ⏎ to calculate the result. The result can then be inserted into the text if desired by pressing **Esc =**, or **Esc $** if a figure is to be in dollar format. For more information on mathematical operations in WordStar, see **Block Operations**,

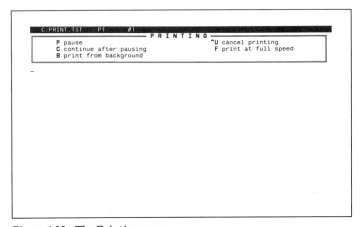

Figure 1.22: The Printing menu

Calculator, **Merge Print**, and **Shorthand** in the Topical Reference section.

The Spelling Check Menu

The Spelling Check menu (Figure 1.24) is accessed by pressing **L**, **N**, or **O** from the Quick menu (**^QL**, **^QN**, or **^QO** from the Edit menu). You can check the spelling of an entire document, of that portion of a document starting from the cursor position, of the word you just typed, or of a word yet to be entered into the document. If you are checking the spelling of more than one word, the Spelling Check menu appears only when WordStar finds a word that does not appear in its dictionaries. When a word that may be misspelled is detected, you can either add one of the numbered suggested replacement words provided by WordStar at the bottom of the menu, ignore that word throughout the document, add it to your personal dictionary, bypass it just once, enter a correction of your own, or replace it throughout the document with another word or corrected spelling of the same one. In Release 4, you can also turn on or off the automatic realignment of paragraphs when a replacement occurs. In Release 5, WordStar also checks for duplicate words, such as "the the," and

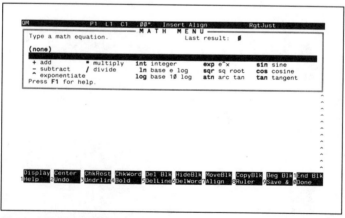

Figure 1.23: The Math menu

displays a definition of the selected word at the bottom of the menu. For more information on the Spelling Check feature, see **Spell** in the Topical Reference section.

The Thesaurus Menu (Release 5)

To access the Thesaurus menu, press **^QJ** from the edit screen. A screen resembling Figure 1.25 will appear with a list of words that are similar or allied in meaning, grouped by parts of speech (noun, verb, and so forth). If more words are listed than will fit on the menu, you can scroll down through the list using the cursor movement keys. From this menu you can choose another word, cancel the operation, enter a new word, look up the definition of a word, cross-reference similar words, or look at words previously selected.

If you choose to look up the definition of a word (either the one you type in the edit screen or one you select from the alternatives), one or several brief definitions will be provided. You can look at the next or previous definition, type in a new word to define, or cancel the operation and return to the regular Thesaurus operation.

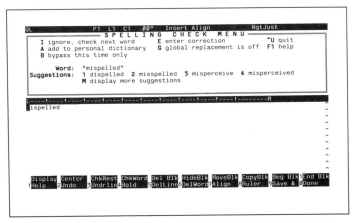

Figure 1.24: The Spelling Check menu

For more information on this feature, see **Thesaurus** in the Topical Reference section.

Word Finder—The Thesaurus (Release 4)

The thesaurus utility provided with WordStar Release 4 is an add-on product to be installed separately and loaded prior to loading WordStar if it is to function properly. It is therefore not actually a menu, but it behaves like one, and so it is included here.

To access Word Finder, press **Alt-1** with the cursor anywhere in the word you want to look up. (As noted before, **Alt-1** works *only* with Release 4; in Release 5 this command has the entirely different function of accessing Page Preview.) A screen will appear resembling Figure 1.26. The word selected will be displayed in the upper-left corner of the screen, and synonyms will be displayed below it in alphabetical order and divided by parts of speech. For example, synonyms for *cry* will be divided into nouns and verbs, since cry can be either. For additional information on Word Finder, see **Thesaurus** in the Topical Reference Section.

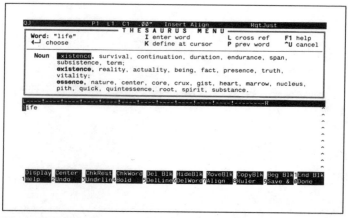

Figure 1.25: The Thesaurus menu, WordStar Release 5

The WordStar Dot Commands

You know that commands can be issued either by pressing a letter (from the Opening menu) or by pressing the Ctrl key and a letter or number in combination (from other menus). Another set of commands in WordStar works along with the menu commands, however, sometimes as alternatives to them, sometimes as additions and refinements, and sometimes as commands that are inserted from the pull-down menus (in Release 5).

These commands are called *dot* commands because they must always begin with a period. They appear in the leftmost column (column 1) of the screen on a line by themselves ending with a hard carriage return. These commands are embedded into the file and are used to save formats for that particular file alone. Some dot commands change the document's appearance on-screen, while others affect only the printed document. They do not affect the default program settings, only those of the file. Since the use of dot commands has changed somewhat from Release 4 to Release 5, here are two separate examples to illustrate the distinction between menu and dot commands.

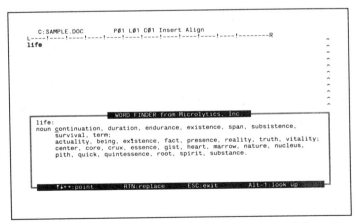

Figure 1.26: A sample Word Finder screen in WordStar Release 4

How Dot Commands Differ from Menu Commands in Release 4: An Example

The following example presents two equivalent commands that govern line spacing. The menu command to set line spacing in WordStar is

^OS [*n*]

where *n* equals the total number of lines including blank ones per line of text (1 = single-spaced, 2 = double-spaced, and so forth). If you press **^OS2** while typing a file, the subsequent paragraphs will be double-spaced. If, however, you close the file, open it again, and type some more text, you must press **^OS2** once more to retain the double-spacing; WordStar doesn't remember that you want the file to be double-spaced. With complicated document formats that are edited frequently, this memory lapse can be annoying.

This is where dot commands come in. To change line spacing with a dot command, use the line spacing dot command:

.LS [*n*]

where *n* equals the total number of lines (including blank ones) per line of text, just like the **^OS** menu command.

Accordingly, if you want double spacing, you would type

.LS2

Now every time the file is edited, WordStar remembers to double-space the document.

How Dot Commands Differ from Menu Commands in Release 5: An Example

The following example presents two roughly equivalent commands that govern paragraph realignment. First, consider the menu command to turn auto-alignment on and off in WordStar:

^OA

If you press **^OA** while typing a file, paragraphs will not be automatically realigned during subsequent editing. If, however, you close the file and open it again, you must press **^OA** once more if you want to resume editing with auto-alignment turned off. WordStar doesn't remember that you want to keep the auto-align feature off. If you have complicated tabular material or you leave the document frequently, this memory lapse can be annoying.

This is where dot commands come in. To turn paragraph realignment off altogether (not just the auto-align feature), use the dot command

.AW OFF

You can turn it back on later on in the document with

.AW ON

Now every time the file is edited, WordStar remembers to turn off paragraph alignment for that section.

Although they are generally a little more complicated to learn, dot commands are more powerful than menu commands, almost a programming language in themselves. In fact, many of WordStar's essential features are available only as dot commands. You will probably find that you can easily memorize the ones you use the most. Explanations of individual dot commands occur throughout the Topical Reference section.

The WordStar Function Keys

The function keys on the IBM PC keyboard are programmed with some of the more frequently used WordStar menu commands. In Release 4, some of these commands are displayed on the bottom two lines of the screen. The top row displays function key commands to be pressed simultaneously with the Shift key, and the bottom row displays those to be pressed alone. There are also function key combinations for the Ctrl and Alt keys. Their functions are not displayed on the screen.

In Release 5, the default option is to have none of the function key assignments displayed on the screen.

The function keys are equivalent to various key combinations in WordStar, and any of them can be programmed by the user using WSCHANGE, WordStar's customizing program, which is described in Appendix A. For a list of all the default function key settings, see the inside front cover.

The WordStar Edit Screen

The part of the user interface most often displayed is the edit screen that you see while typing. The standard edit screen for WordStar Release 5 appears in Figure 1.27. You may find the amount of information displayed is unnecessary or distracting. Since people have different needs from their word processors, WordStar allows you to choose just how much information you want displayed by adjusting the help level settings, WSCHANGE, and the Onscreen Format menu. For more information on the edit screen, see **Help** and **Ruler Line** in the Topical Reference section, and Appendix A.

The Status Line

The Status Line is the line of information at the top of your screen. It displays the name of your file (as well as the drive it is on) at the left side, the current page, line, and column in the middle, and additional information about the status of toggle commands at the right side, such as whether text typed is inserted into existing text (in which case the word "Insert" appears on the line) or replaces it, whether the document is protected, whether column mode is on or off, whether Preview is on (in Release 4), and so forth. If you find this information distracting or want more room on the screen to be devoted to text, use help level 0 (press ^JJ0↵) from either the Opening or Edit screens).

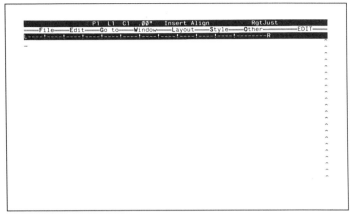

Figure 1.27: The WordStar Edit screen

The Menu Bar (Release 5)

In Release 5 of WordStar, the next line you see is the menu bar, a line that shows the pull-down menus you can access by pressing the Alt key in combination with the highlighted first letter of each menu. If you don't use the pull-down menus, you can eliminate the menu bar from the screen by setting your help level to 3 or less.

The Ruler Line

The ruler line is the line on your screen that displays the margin and tab settings currently in use, and looks something like this:

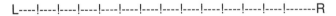

L----!----!----!----!----!----!----!----!----!----!----!----!----!-------R

Ruler lines can also be set into the text to retain settings within a document when you return to it. The meaning of each of the characters along the ruler line is listed below.

L   Left margin

-    One column space

!   Tab stop

#	Decimal tab stop (used to align numbers vertically along a column)
P	Paragraph margin
R	Right margin
V	Temporary indent

The Flag Column

The flag column is the rightmost column of the screen in WordStar. It displays information about the corresponding horizontal line of text. The following is a list of the characters you will find in the flag column along with their meanings.

(blank)	Soft carriage return
<	Line ends with hard carriage return
B	Block begins on line (Release 4 only)
C	Column break (Release 5 only)
F	Line ends in form feed
J	Line ends with line feed, no carriage return
K	Block ends on line (Release 4 only)
P	Page break here
?	Unrecognized dot command
-	Carriage return, no line feed; line will be over-printed by next line
+	Line extends past rightmost column of screen
1	Dot command changes printed page and screen appearance; should be at beginning of file
.	Dot command changes printed page and screen

: Dot command changes printed page only

^ End of file

Note: In Release 5, marked blocks are indicated by highlighting the flag column for each line in the block, instead of by a B and K in the flag columns.

PART II

Topical Reference

Abandon

See **Save**.

Align Paragraphs

These commands realign paragraphs after editing or changing margins.

RELEASE

4 and 5

KEY SEQUENCE

To align a single paragraph:

^B

or

F7

or (in Release 5 only):

EDIT/Layout/Align rest of paragraph

To align the rest of a document:

^QU

or (in Release 5 only):

EDIT/Layout/Align rest of document

While editing files, it is often necessary to realign the margins of paragraphs because of deletions or additions on a line or changes of margin or justification settings. WordStar Release 4 does not automatically adjust paragraphs every time a deletion or addition is made. Release 5 realigns automatically unless you change the margin or justification settings. To realign a single paragraph with your current settings, place your cursor on the line where changes were made and press **^B** or **F7**. Pressing **F7** instead of **^B** in Release 5 also moves the cursor back to the beginning of that paragraph. If you are using hyphen help (**^OH**), the automatic hyphenation function in Release 4, WordStar will pause to allow you to decide where to hyphenate suggested words. If you are using the auto-hyphenation feature in Release 5, hyphens will be inserted automatically.

If you need to realign more than one paragraph or your entire document (to adjust to a wider margin setting, for instance), move your cursor to the top of the section that you want to align and press **^QU**. This will realign all the paragraphs in the document. To stop the **^QU** operation, press **^U**.

Preserving Special Alignment

This dot command turns off realignment, right-justification, and word wrap temporarily.

KEY SEQUENCE

.AW OFF
<text whose alignment is to be preserved>
.AW ON

USAGE	

If your document has tabular material or paragraphs with special indention you want to preserve, use the **.AW OFF** command to prevent the **^QU** or **^B** paragraph alignment commands from realigning these sections of text improperly. If you use **^B**, the cursor will not advance past the **.AW OFF** command. You must use the cursor movement keys to do so. When regular text with standard paragraphs resumes, use the **.AW ON** command to turn the paragraph alignment feature back on.

Paragraph Alignment with Merge Printing

This dot command governs how WordStar aligns or does not align text while merge printing.

KEY SEQUENCE	

To align only text that contains inserted data variables:

.PF DIS
<Text to be aligned>

To realign every paragraph:

.PF ON
<Text to be aligned>

To turn automatic realignment off:

.PF OFF
<Text>

USAGE

To realign paragraphs while merge printing a document, use the **.PF** command. This command has three settings. The default setting is **.PF DIS** (for discretionary). This setting causes WordStar to realign only the paragraphs that have text inserted as data variables and leaves the other paragraphs alone. The **.PF ON** setting realigns every paragraph. The **.PF OFF** setting turns the automatic realignment of paragraphs off during merge printing, which can be useful when sections of text exceed the margin but should not wrap around to the next line. All of the settings mentioned can be used within one document.

SEE ALSO

Auto-Align

Column Alignment

Annotations

See **Notes**.

Append

See **Block Operations: Write Block.**

ASCII Conversion

WordStar offers two methods of converting files from its own Document storage mode to the industry standard ASCII mode.

RELEASE

4 and 5

KEY SEQUENCE

To convert characters to ASCII and all soft carriage returns to hard carriage returns from the Opening menu:

N<*filename.ext* >
^QU

or (in Release 5 only), from the Opening menu:

File/Open a nondocument file... <*filename.ext* > ⏎
Edit/Layout/Align rest of document

To convert file to ASCII by printing to disk, in Release 4, from the Opening menu:

P<*filename.ext* > ⏎
Number of copies?
Pause between pages (Y/N) ?
Use form feeds (Y/N)   ?
Starting page   ?
Ending page   ?
Nondocument (Y/N)   ?
Name of printer   ? ASCII > <*filename.ext* >

To convert file to ASCII by printing to disk, in Release 5:

File/Print a file...
Printer name **ASCII**
Redirect output to *<filename.ext>*

USAGE ════════════════════

ASCII is an acronym for American Standard Code for Information Interchange. When data is stored using this code, it can be interpreted by another computer or program. Word-Star nondocument mode stores files in this manner, but the document mode does not. There are two methods to convert document files to ASCII: realigning in nondocument mode and printing to a disk file.

If you have a document file with no document formatting or print formatting codes and you want to convert it to ASCII format, or if you have a document file with or without formatting codes that you want to convert to WordStar nondocument format, use the first method. First, open the file with **N** instead of **D** from the Opening menu (or from the pull-down File menu in Release 5). Next, press either **^B** repeatedly (to reformat the file one line at a time) or **^QU** (to reformat the file all at once). This operation will switch the top bit in WordStar's document format (that is, it changes that aspect of the document mode's storage format that differs from the ASCII standard). Note that this operation will also replace all soft carriage returns (carriage returns inserted automatically by WordStar in document mode when a line wraps) with hard carriage returns, rendering word wrap useless. Make a copy of the file first if you intend to edit the file later in document mode.

If you don't need to preserve print control codes, if you are using variables in your document, if you want to keep soft carriage returns, or if you are saving this file to be read by another word processing program, use the second method. If you do not specify a new file name, WordStar will assign the name ASCII.WS to the new file automatically. In Release 4 you must use the > operator before the new file name.

SEE ALSO

Nondocument Mode
Print

Auto-Align

The Auto-Align switch turns automatic realignment of
paragraphs during editing on and off.

RELEASE

5 only

KEY SEQUENCE

^OA

USAGE

Release 5 of WordStar automatically realigns your current
paragraph as you are editing. If you find this distracting, you
can turn the feature off or on by pressing **^OA**. If you want
to change the default setting for this feature to off or change
the amount of time WordStar waits before each realignment,
use WSCHANGE, described in Appendix A.

SEE ALSO

Align Paragraphs

Auto Indent

Auto Indent is used in nondocument mode to indent programming lines automatically. In document mode, the key sequence listed below performs a different operation; see **Hard Return Conversion.**

RELEASE

4 and 5

KEY SEQUENCE

^6

USAGE

Auto Indent is primarily designed for programmers to make it easier to show the structure of their code by indention. To use this feature, indent the first line of the section of code you want to indent with either the Tab key or Spacebar, and then press ^6. The words "Auto-In" will appear on the status line, and the following lines you type will be indented to the same place as the previous line. You can return to the previous level of indention by moving the cursor to the left of the indent. The next line you type will have the new indent.

SEE ALSO

Nondocument Mode

Backup

See **Save.**

Block Operations

Blocks of text can be marked in WordStar to be copied, moved, deleted, written to a separate file, lowercased, upper-cased, or totaled. In WordStar Release 5, they can also be moved or copied from one window to another.

RELEASE

4 and 5

KEY SEQUENCE

   ^KB<*text* >**^KK**

or

   Shift-F9<*text* >**Shift-F10**

or (in Release 5 only):

   EDIT/Edit/Begin block<*text* >EDIT/Edit/End block

USAGE

To mark a block of text, you must mark both the beginning (with **^KB**) and end (with **^KK**). When you mark the beginning of a block, you will see the code <B> displayed in inverse video (or an alternate color if you have a color monitor) on your screen. When you mark the end of the block, the entire block will appear highlighted in inverse video (or an alternate color), the end markers <B> and <K> will disappear.

If you are marking a column block, you must mark the upper-left corner with the beginning marker and the lower-right corner with the end marker.

SEE ALSO

Case Conversion

Go To

Sort

Block Math

The Block Math feature can be used to sum lists of numbers within your WordStar document.

KEY SEQUENCE

^KB<*list of numbers* >**^KK ^KM**

or

Shift-F9<*list of numbers* >**Shift-F10 ^KM**

or (in Release 5 only):

EDIT/Edit/Begin block<*list of numbers* >
EDIT/Edit/End block
EDIT/Other/Block math (add numbers)

USAGE

When a simple list of numbers has been marked as a block, this command sums all the numbers. The block can be in either regular or column mode. Text occurring within the block will be ignored by WordStar, including currency symbols such as $ and £. A hyphen immediately preceding a number will be understood as negative, as will numbers immediately enclosed in parentheses (that is, without spaces). Commas within a number will be ignored. Numbers need only be separated by a single space when aligned horizontally. The letter e (either upper- or lowercase) can be used to signify scientific notation; thus, 2e8 would be understood as 2×10^8, or 200,000,000.

A number must be no longer than 30 digits to be understood by WordStar; otherwise, it must be approximately represented in scientific notation. Calculations in WordStar have a precision of 12 decimal places. If the calculation gives a larger result, WordStar will give the nearest approximate answer it can in scientific notation.

SEE ALSO

Calculator

Merge Print

Column Block

The Column Block feature is used to mark vertical columns of text for block operations. It is a toggle command.

KEY SEQUENCE

^KN

or (in Release 5 only):

EDIT/Edit/Column block mode

USAGE

To perform a block operation on a vertical column of text (a rectangular block), first turn Column Block mode on by pressing ^KN. The word "Column" appears on the status line. Then mark the beginning of the column block by pressing ^KB in the top left corner of the block and mark the end by pressing ^KK in the bottom right corner. You can then perform any of the block operations.

SEE ALSO

Block Operations: Column Replace

Column Replace

Column Replace allows you to replace a column with another column.

KEY SEQUENCE

^KI

or (in Release 5 only):

EDIT/Edit/Column replace mode

USAGE

To replace one column block with another, use this command in conjunction with Column Block (^KN); it will not function in standard block mode. Press ^KI and the word "ColRepl" will appear on the status line. Mark the column you want to move, move the cursor to the top left corner of the column you want to replace, and then press **^KV**. If you want to perform this operation and keep the originally marked column intact, follow the same steps but use **^KC** (Copy Block) instead of **^KV**.

TIP

If the column being replaced is longer or wider than the new column, the extra characters will still be on the screen. To eliminate this problem, mark a column block large enough to completely cover the original by adding blank space to the right and below (or above) the replacing column. The marked blank space will replace the existing extra characters when you perform the replacement.

SEE ALSO

Block Operations: Column Block
                   Column Replace
                   Move Block

Copy Block

Copy block copies a marked block of text to the location of the cursor at the time the command is issued. In Release 5, you can also copy a block from one window to another.

KEY SEQUENCE

To copy a block within one file:

^KC

or

Shift-F8

or (in Release 5 only):

   EDIT/Edit/Copy block

To copy a block from one window to another (Release 5 only):

   ^KA

or

   EDIT/Window/Copy block from other window

USAGE

To copy a block within a file, mark the block using **^KB** and **^KK**, move the cursor to the place where the text is to be inserted, and press **^KC**. The block will be inserted at the cursor position. The original block will still be marked, and you should hide the block (**^KH**) if you are finished with your copy operation because cursor movement is slowed somewhat if a block is marked. To copy one block many times in a row, combine **^KC** with the Repeat command.

   To copy a block from one window to another, mark the block in the source window, and then press **^OK** to go to the other window. Position the cursor where you want the block to be copied, and then press **^KA**.

TIP

Here's a shortcut to copying smaller blocks of text: take advantage of WordStar's undo command (^U). This command will restore any deleted text (up to 500 bytes). To use ^U for copying text, first delete the text you want to copy using any of the standard delete commands except Del, Backspace, or ^G (^U will not restore a single-character deletion). Then press ^U to restore the original section of text you deleted. Now move your cursor to the place where you want the copy to be inserted, taking care not to use any delete commands in the process. Press ^U once more. WordStar remembers the last section of text deleted and restores it at the new location in your document.

Since there is always the chance of accidentally using a delete command, this method is not recommended for sections of text too large to recall if you make a mistake. This technique cannot be used to copy blocks from one window to another because WordStar maintains separate undo buffers for each window.

SEE ALSO

Block Operations: Column Block
                    Move Block
                    Repeat
                    Undo

Delete Block

This command deletes a standard or column block.

KEY SEQUENCE

^KY

or

Shift-F5

or (in Release 5 only):

EDIT/Edit/Delete block

USAGE

To delete a block of text, first mark the beginning of the block with **^KB** and the end of the block with **^KK**. When you have marked the block and the text is highlighted, press **^KY** to delete the block. If the block contains fewer than 500 bytes, you can restore it with **^U**, but only if you have deleted nothing else since deleting the block. WordStar will let you know the block is too large to restore at the time of deletion.

Display/Hide Block

Block markers and place markers can be displayed or hidden but not removed; this command displays or hides them.

KEY SEQUENCE
---

^KH

or

Shift-F6

or (in Release 5 only):

EDIT/Edit/Hide/show block

USAGE

WordStar shows a marked block in inverse video (or an alternate color if you are using a color monitor), and you may find the display distracting and want to turn it off. Also, operations that are displayed on-screen take longer to execute if a block is marked. For these reasons, WordStar allows you to hide a block using **^KH**. This turns the marked block off, as well as any place markers. The block and place markers will be retained in memory, however, and can be retrieved by pressing **^KH** once more to reverse the operation.

No block operations can be performed while block markers are hidden (unless you have set the help level to 0 in Release 5), but new markers can be set at any time, replacing those already set.

SEE ALSO

Markers

Move Block

Blocks can be moved from one location to the cursor position in WordStar. In Release 5, blocks can also be moved from one window to another.

KEY SEQUENCE

To move a block:

^KV

or

Shift-F7

or (in Release 5 only):

EDIT/Edit/Move block

To move a block from one window to another (Release 5 only):

^KG

or

EDIT/Window/Move block from other window

USAGE

To move a block of text, first mark the block using **^KB** and **^KK**. Next, position the cursor where you want to place the block of text. Then press **^KV** to move the block from its original position in your document to the position of your cursor. Reformat the text in its new position as necessary using ^B or ^QU. WordStar does not do this automatically.

To move a block from one window to another, mark the block in the source window, and then press ^OK to go to the other window. Position the cursor where you want the block to be moved, and then press ^KG.

When moving blocks of text, WordStar is always in Insert mode (except when Column Replace is on). That is, a block of text will never obliterate existing text. It always pushes it forward instead.

SEE ALSO

Block Operations: Copy Block
Column Replace

Read Block

This command inserts an existing text file or, in Release 5, a specified range from a dBASE database or a Lotus 1-2-3, Symphony, or Quattro spreadsheet into your document.

KEY SEQUENCE

^KR <*d:\pathname\filename.ext* > ↵

or (in Release 5 only):

EDIT/Edit/Insert a file...
<*d:\pathname\filename.ext* > ↵

USAGE

To insert an entire existing file into the one you are currently working in, position your cursor at the point where you want the file to be inserted, and then press ^KR. You will be prompted to specify a file name. You can include a drive and path (directory) in this specification.

If you have Release 5, you can select a dBASE database or spreadsheet in Lotus 1-2-3, Symphony, or Quattro. If you select a spreadsheet, WordStar will display a dialog box showing the entire cell range of that file. Using the standard editing keys, you can specify a smaller cell range within the spreadsheet. When you have finished selecting a range, press ^K or **F10**. The cell range will be inserted into your WordStar file as straight text.

Write Block

This command copies a marked block to a new file. In Release 5, you also have the option to append the block to the end of an existing file.

KEY SEQUENCE

^KW *<d:\pathname\filename.ext >* ↵

or (in Release 5 only):

EDIT/Edit/Write block to file...
<d:\pathname\filename.ext >↵

USAGE

To copy a block to a new file, first mark the block using **^KB** and **^KK**, and then press **^KW**. You will be prompted to specify a file name. You can include a drive and path (directory) in this specification.

To append a block to the end of an existing file, follow the same procedure as described above. When you specify an existing file name, you will see the following message:

File already exists. Overwrite (Y/N) or append (A)?

Press **A** to append the block to the end of the file, **Y** to over-write the existing file (thereby eliminating it) or **N** to aban-don the operation.

Binding Space

This command inserts a space that will not allow the two words it separates to split at the end of a line.

RELEASE

4 and 5

KEY SEQUENCE

*<firstword >***^PO***<secondword >***^PO***<thirdword >etc.*

USAGE

Binding spaces are especially useful for dates—January 13, 1990—and names—Da Vinci—that you don't want to see separated by word wrap. To insert a binding space, type the first word, and then press **^PO**. If you have control codes hid-den, it will appear as a simple space. If you have control codes displayed, a **^O** will appear instead in Release 4, and a solid box (■) in Release 5. The next word you type will not be separated from the first one unless you press ↵ between them or delete the binding space.

SEE ALSO

Hide/Display Controls

Boldface

This command turns boldface printing on and off.

RELEASE

4 and 5

KEY SEQUENCE

^PB<*text* >**^PB**

or

F4<*text* >F4

or (in Release 5 only):

EDIT/Style/Bold<*text* >EDIT/Style/Bold

USAGE

To print boldface text, press **^PB** where you want the boldface to begin, and **^PB** once more where you want it to end. If you have control codes hidden, the text that you have boldfaced will appear brighter or in a different color. If you have control codes displayed, ^B markers will appear where you inserted the codes as well. To remove boldfacing, simply delete the codes. Boldfacing can be combined with other print controls such as underlining or italics, although your printer may not be capable of printing all combinations.

SEE ALSO

Hide/Display Controls

Box Drawing

See **Graphics Characters**.

Calculator

This command allows you to perform mathematical operations and enter either the results or the equations into the document.

RELEASE

4 and 5

KEY SEQUENCE

To access the calculator (alternatively called the Math menu):

^QM

or (in Release 5 only):

EDIT/Other/Calculator...

To insert the last result into the text:

Esc=

or (in Release 5 only):

EDIT/Other/Shorthand macros.../=

To insert the last result in dollar and cents format:

Esc$

or (in Release 5 only):

EDIT/Other/Shorthand macros.../$

To insert the last equation into the text:

Esc#

or (in Release 5 only):

EDIT/Other/Shorthand macros.../#

USAGE

To use the Calculator, first use the key sequence above; next, type in the calculation you want to perform, and then press ↵. Arithmetical operations can be performed by typing the equation. For example, typing **4+7**↵ yields the result 11. The arithmetic operators that you can use are

- `+`   add
- `−`   subtract
- `*`   multiply
- `/`   divide
- `^`   exponentiate

To calculate logarithmic, trigonometric, and other mathematical functions, type the name of the function and then the value to be operated on by the function enclosed in parentheses, making sure that there is no space between the function and the parentheses. For example, typing **sqr(81)**↵ will yield the result 9. The mathematical functions that operate in this manner are

atn(x)	arctangent
cos(x)	cosine
exp(x)	e^x, where $e = 2.71828$
int(x)	integer
log	base 10 logarithm
ln	base e logarithm
sin	sine
sqr	square root
tan	tangent

Exponential calculations are performed first, followed by multiplication and division, followed by addition and subtraction. To change the precedence of calculations, you can use parentheses, as in standard mathematical notation. The maximum number of pairs of parentheses in WordStar is 32.

For very large numbers, scientific notation can be used. To enter a number in this manner, use e. (Don't confuse this e, which stands for 10 raised to the specified power, with the e of the logarithmic and exponentiation functions noted above.) For example, to express the number 100 in scientific notation, (1×10^2), type **1e2**. WordStar has a precision of 12 decimal places, and any result with more decimal places required will be approximated in scientific notation, up to 1×10^{63} or 1×10^{-63}.

To insert a result or equation into the text, leave the calculator by pressing ^U and move the cursor to the point at which you want the result or equation inserted; then press **Esc** and the corresponding character, as shown above in the key sequence. The $ option (which converts results to numbers in dollar format) can be customized to another currency format if you so choose. See Appendix A for more details.

SEE ALSO

Block Operations: Block Math

Case Conversion

This command changes the case (upper- or lowercase) of the letters in a marked block of text.

RELEASE

4 and 5

KEY SEQUENCE

To convert all text in a block to lowercase:

   ^KB
   <text to be converted>
   ^KK
   ^K'

or

   Shift-F9
   <text to be converted>
   Shift-F10
   ^K'

or (in Release 5 only):

   EDIT/Edit/Begin block
   <text to be converted>
   EDIT/Edit/End block
   ^K'

To convert all text in a block to uppercase:

   ^KB
   <text to be converted>
   ^KK
   ^K"

or

   Shift-F9
   <text to be converted>
   Shift-F10
   ^K"

or (in Release 5 only):

EDIT/Edit/Begin block
<text to be converted >
EDIT/Edit/End block
^K"

To convert the first letter of each sentence in a block to upper-case and the rest of the letters to lowercase (in Release 5 only):

^KB
<text to be converted >
^KK
^K.

or

Shift-F9
<text to be converted >
Shift-F10
^K.

or

EDIT/Edit/Begin block
<text to be converted >
EDIT/Edit/End block
^K.

USAGE

To convert the case of a block of text, first mark the block (it can be either a standard or a column block), and then press **^K** and either ' to lowercase, " to uppercase, or, in Release 5, . to uppercase the first letter of each sentence and lowercase the rest. The case conversion does not include other charac-ters; the $ symbol, for example, will not be converted to a 4.

Exercise care using the case conversion commands, espe-cially the uppercase command, because once you have con-verted all letters to uppercase, you cannot reconvert them to lowercase without reconverting the first letter of each sentence and proper nouns as well. In Release 5, you can then convert the beginnings of sentences back to uppercase, but any other words that were originally capitalized or all uppercase will remain lowercase.

Centering

These commands allow you to center a line or lines of text horizontally or vertically on the page.

RELEASE

4 and 5

KEY SEQUENCE

To center a line of text horizontally:

^OC

or

Shift-F2

or (in Release 5 only):

EDIT/Layout/Center line

To turn horizontal centering on or off (in Release 5 only):

.OC ON/OFF

To center text vertically on a page (in Release 5 only):

^OV

USAGE

To center a single line of text horizontally in WordStar, press **^OC** with your cursor anywhere within the text to be centered.

WordStar inserts the appropriate amount of space to the left of the text until it is centered on the line. In Release 5, you will see a rightward-pointing arrow (➤) in column one to indicate the centering is created by an indent. This works only for text already typed on a line ending in a hard carriage return (↵). To remove centering from a single line, position the cursor at the left margin and press **^T** or press **^G** or **Del** until you have deleted the space. If you change the left or right margins, reissue the **^OC** command for the new margins.

In Release 5, text typed in below the **.OC ON** dot command will be centered, provided each line of text ends with a hard carriage return (↵). To turn centering off for the remainder of a document, insert the dot command **.OC OFF**. To center several lines of existing text, insert **.OC ON** on a line above the text and then reformat the text using **^B** or **^QU**. You can bring the text flush with the left margin again by removing the centering code and reformatting the text using the same command.

To center continuous text vertically (in Release 5 only), position the cursor on the first line of text you want to center on the page and press **^OV**. Blank lines will be inserted above the text and a page break command (.PA) will be inserted at the end of the text to center it on the page. WordStar's calculations of the center of the page take into account your current page length, header, footer, top, and bottom margins settings.

SEE ALSO

Margins

Character Count

This command displays the number of bytes contained in the file from the beginning of the file up to (but not including) the cursor position.

RELEASE

4 and 5

KEY SEQUENCE

^Q?

USAGE

The character count feature can be very useful in determining the size of your document or finding your place in a longer document. Press ^Q? and WordStar will give you the number of bytes in your file up to the location of your cursor. This roughly corresponds to the number of characters plus any codes. In Release 5, there are always at least 128 bytes of codes at the beginning of the file. Press **Esc** to return to editing.

SEE ALSO

Word Count

Character Width

This command allows you to set the width and spacing of each character on the page.

RELEASE

4 and 5

KEY SEQUENCE

.CW *n*

where *n* is the character width in 120ths of an inch.

USAGE

WordStar defines *character width* as the width of the character plus the small space that separates it from the next character. With nonproportional fonts, this sum is a uniform amount. With proportional fonts, the character width varies with each character since the space between them is uniform but the width of each character (compare the size of *m* and *i*) is not. In this case, the character width command determines the *average* character width.

The behavior of the character width command depends largely on the capabilities of your printer. Printing the file PRINT.TST that comes with WordStar will enable you to determine what spacing and font your printer will use for each character width. Here is a summary of how the character width command affects various types of printers.

If you have a daisy-wheel printer, you are limited to one or perhaps two sizes of characters, usually pica and elite. With this type of printer, the command determines only the distance between characters. If you have a dot-matrix printer, the command may also determine the size of characters, or font size, as well as spacing. With laser printers, the character width command determines font size and can also affect the spacing between characters.

If you often use two specific fonts (or *pitches*, with a daisy-wheel printer), you can set the character width defaults for each one in WSCHANGE and switch between fonts using the Alternate (^**PA**) and Normal Pitch (^**PN**) control codes. See **Pitch** and Appendix A for more details.

If you have Release 5, using the Choose font feature is a much more effective way to control the size of print on the page; use the character width command for fine tuning adjustments. See **Choose Font** for more details.

To set the character width, insert the dot command **.CW** followed by the width in 120ths of an inch. The default setting is 10 characters per inch (12/120 inch). To set the character width to 12 characters per inch (10/120 inch), you would insert

.CW 10

on a line above any text you wanted have this new character width.

SEE ALSO

Choose Font

Pitch

Choose Font

This command allows you to select a font from a list of those available for your printer. It then inserts a font tag into your document.

RELEASE

5 only

KEY SEQUENCE

^P=<*font name*>↵

or

EDIT/Style/Choose font...
<*font name*>↵

USAGE

To select a font, press one of the key sequences listed above. After you have pressed **^P=** or selected **Choose font**, a dialog box will appear showing the name of the font currently in use and below it a list of available fonts for your printer. The font name consists of a coded abbreviation of the style and size of the font.

If the font is *nonproportional* (allowing each character the same amount of space on a page, like a typewriter), the size will be measured in *pitch*, that is, in characters per inch. For example, a daisy-wheel printer might have a nonproportional font of COURIER 10, meaning 10-pitch (10 characters per inch) in Courier typeface.

If the font is *proportional* (allowing more space for a wide letter such as *m* and less for a narrow letter such as *i*, as in typeset text), the size will be measured in points (a printing measurement that is approximately 1/72 inch). For example, you might have have a laser printer that has 12-point Helvetica. This would appear as HELVETICA 12.

To select a font from the list, either type in the code from the list or use the cursor keys to move into the list and highlight the desired font. Then press ↵. The edit screen will reappear with the font tag inserted in bright letters between angle brackets in your document, like this:

<COURIER 10>

You can delete a font tag just as you would regular text.

If you select a different printer from the one whose fonts you chose while editing the document, WordStar will attempt to approximate the fonts chosen for the original printer. For best results, however, select the new printer using **^P?**, and then replace the old font tags with those the new printer is capable of producing. You can find font tags in a document by pressing **^Q=** or selecting **EDIT/Go to/Go to next font**.

SEE ALSO

Go To

Pitch

Color, Selecting Screen

See **Appendix A.**

Color Printing (Release 5 Only)

(For Release 4, *see* **Italics/Color.**)

This command inserts a command tag to print in any of 16 colors, if the printer is capable of color printing.

KEY SEQUENCE

^P-<*color* >↵

USAGE

To select printing colors for a color printer, press **^P-** and a dialog box will appear showing the current or default color to print with. A list of 16 colors will appear at the bottom of the screen. To choose a new color, type the new color's name over the default color or use the cursor movement keys to highlight the color in the list and then press ↵. The edit screen will reappear with a command tag inserted into the text in bright letters enclosed in angle brackets, like this:

<Light Blue>

Some types of laser printers can use this command to print in patterns or in reverse (white on black). Consult your printer's documentation for more information.

SEE ALSO

Italics/Color

Appendix A

Column Alignment

These commands ensure alignment of tabular columns on the printed document.

RELEASE

4 and 5

KEY SEQUENCE

See individual sections.

USAGE

When working with tabular material in WordStar, you will occasionally encounter a row of text or numbers that aligns perfectly well on the screen but prints out with a ragged left edge for no apparent reason. There are, however, two reasons for the ragged alignment, and each has a solution.

Alignment by Disabling Microjustification

This command allows you to eliminate misalignment caused by microjustification.

KEY SEQUENCE

To turn microjustification off:

.UJ OFF

or

.UJ 0

To resume microjustification:

.UJ ON

or

.UJ 1

USAGE

Some printers (most daisy-wheel printers, for instance) have the capability of inserting between words spaces that are less than one character space wide. This is called *microjustification*. By inserting these spaces, the printer can make each line more even in length and hence more pleasing to the eye. WordStar takes advantage of this capability unless you tell it otherwise. Unfortunately, these extra spaces often cause ragged left edges when you print tables. To prevent raggedness, insert the dot command to turn off microjustification, **.UJ OFF** (or **.UJ 0**).

Using the Fixed Position Character with Proportional Spacing

This command allows you to align proportionally spaced text on a specific column.

KEY SEQUENCE

^P@<*text to align* >

USAGE

Typewriters, most dot-matrix printers, and daisy-wheel printers treat each character as if it were the same width, creating more space around an *i* than an *m*, for example. This is called *monospacing* or *nonproportional spacing*. If you have a laser printer, however, or some types of dot-matrix printer, you can use print fonts that space the letters proportionally, creating printed material that resembles mechanical typesetting. This is called *proportional spacing*. While proportional spacing improves the look of your document, it is often difficult to print vertically-aligned columns. WordStar has found a solution to this problem with the fixed position control code, **^P@**.

For example, if you want to align the right column of the price list below using a proportionally spaced font, position the cursor at the dollar sign in *$3.25*.

```
Apples      $3.25
Oranges     $2.49
Kiwi fruit  $4.08
```

Press **^P@**. You will see the **^@** code to the left of the dollar sign. Repeat the operation at the left edge of the entire column until it appears on-screen as shown below:

```
Apples      ^@$3.25
Oranges     ^@$2.49
Kiwi fruit  ^@$4.08
```

Your printed document will now print aligned, just as you see it on-screen. (If you find the **^@** code distracting, you can turn the print controls display off by pressing **^OD**. The codes will still be in your document; you just won't see them on-screen.)

SEE ALSO

Proportional Spacing

Columns

These commands allow you to generate newspaper-style columns in WordStar.

RELEASE

5 only

KEY SEQUENCE

To turn on newspaper columns:

.CO *n,g*

where *n* is the number of columns (from 1 to 8) and *g* the width of the *gutter* (the space between columns).

To keep lines together in the same column:

.CC *n*

where *n* is the number of lines to be kept in the same column.

To start a new column before the end of the page:

.CB

USAGE

To use newspaper columns in a document, you must first decide on the width you want for the column. The column width is determined by the current settings for the left and right margins. Use either an embedded ruler line (see **Ruler Line**) or the .RM right margin setting command (see **Margins**) to adjust the width of the column.

For example, if your current settings are a left margin at column 1 and a right margin at 65, or 6.40 in. (WordStar's default setting), and you want to have two columns with a 5-space gutter between them, set your right margin at 30 (2.90 in.) either by inserting the command

.RM 30

or

.RM 2.90"

or by embedding a ruler line with an R at column 30, like this one:

.RR- - ! - - - - ! - - - - ! - - - - ! - - - - ! - - -R

Now insert the command

.CO 2,5

to begin two columns with a 5-space gutter. *The total number of columns times the column width plus the total gutter space should equal the width between the left and right page margins.* Inches can be used instead of column numbers for both the right margin and columns dot commands, if you find this easier, by adding an inch mark (") after the number in the dot command (for example: **.CO 2,.5"**).

You must use this command with care. When you insert **.RM** and **.CO** above existing text, you must reformat that text with **^QU** or it will retain its former width on the screen. On the Page Preview screen the columns will appear to overlap.

After you type the column dot command, a triple bar (≡) appears in the left margin of each line in reverse video or a different color, depending on your monitor type. When you reach the end of the page, a column break appears (a line resembling a page break, except that it is a double line and there is a C in the flag column) and two triple bars appear in the left margin (≡≡) to signify that you are now typing in the second column. The columns do not appear side-by-side on the regular edit screen, but you can see how they will actually appear when printed by using Page Preview (**^OP** or **Alt-1**), if you have a graphics monitor and sufficient memory.

To keep certain lines together in the same column (like a numbered list of items, for instance), use the dot command **.CC** and the number of lines you want to keep together. The following lines specified will remain in the same column during further editing, even if you add or delete text from the column.

To start a new column before you reach the end of a page, use the dot command **.CB**. This inserts a column break and starts you at the top of the next column. If the command is inserted on the last column of the page, it will start you on the first column of the next page. If you want to have newspaper columns of equal depth that do not run to the bottom of the page, use this same command, making sure to insert it at the same line number for each column.

To turn off newspaper columns, insert a **.CO 1** or **.CO** command in the file and add a full page right margin again. If you want to change existing text back into standard single column format, remove the column dot commands (**.CO**, **.CB**, and **.CC**), readjust the ruler line or right margin codes, and then reformat the text using **^QU** or **^B**.

SEE ALSO

Column Alignment

Margins

Page Preview

Ruler Lines

Command Files

Command files consist entirely of dot commands and perform a number of print commands in sequence.

RELEASE ═══════════

4 and 5

KEY SEQUENCE ═══════════

To run a command file with no merge variables from the Opening menu:

P *<command file name>*

or in Release 5 only, using the pull-down menus:

File/Print a file...
<command file name>

To run a command file with no merge variables from the Edit menu in Release 4:

^KP N *<command file name>*

To run a command file with no merge variables from the Edit menu in Release 5:

^KPP *<command file name>*

or

EDIT/File/Print a file...
<command file name>

To run a command file with merge variables from the Classic Opening menu:

M *<command file name>*

or in Release 5, using the pull-down menus:

File/Merge print a file...
<command file name>

To run a command file with merge variables from the Edit menu in Release 4:

^KP Y *<command file name>*

To run a command file with merge variables from the Edit menu in Release 5:

^KPM *<command file name>*

or

EDIT/File/Merge print a file...
<command file name>

USAGE

Command files are used to merge files or print several files in a row. To create a command file, open a file in the usual manner and enter the dot commands you want performed. Save the file and run it, using either one of the Print commands listed above (if there are no merge variables) or one of the Merge Print commands (if merge variables are involved). The following are dot commands commonly used in command files. Commands specifically relating to merge printing are discussed in the **Merge Print** entry.

Clear Screen

This command clears the screen and temporarily halts printing to display a message of your choice.

KEY SEQUENCE

.CS *<message>*

USAGE

To have the screen cleared and the message of your choosing appear on the screen, insert this dot command into a command file. It is useful for letting you know when a part of your command file has been executed. In Release 5, a beep will sound to let you know there is a message.

If you are using background printing, the message will not be visible unless you switch to the Printing menu (press **P** or select **File/Print a file...** from the Opening menu or press **^KP** or select **EDIT/File/Print a file...** if you are editing another file).

Display Message

This command displays the message of your choice on the Printing menu.

KEY SEQUENCE

   .DM <*message*>

USAGE

To display a message on the Printing menu while printing a file, use this command. It differs from the Clear Screen (**.CS**) command in that it doesn't halt the printing operation or clear the screen to display the message.

If you are using background printing, the message will not be visible unless you switch to the Printing menu (press **P** or select **File/Print a file...** from the Opening menu or press **^KP** or select **EDIT/File/Print a file...** if you are editing another file).

Insert a File

This command allows you to begin printing the specified file from within your command file.

KEY SEQUENCE

.**FI** *<d:\pathname\filename.ext >*

USAGE

To combine documents while printing, use the dot command
.**FI** in a command file. If you are using several of these commands in a list to create a *print queue* (a list of separate documents to be printed all in a row) and want each document to
begin at the top of a new page and start page numbering at
1, you should insert hard page breaks at the end of each file
(.**PA**) and page numbering commands set to 1 (.**PN1**) at the
beginning of each file.

SEE ALSO

Merge Print

Print

Comments

These commands allow you to insert comments into your
files that appear on-screen but will not be printed.

RELEASE

4 and 5

| KEY SEQUENCE |

To insert a one-line comment:

  ..<*comment* >

or

  .IG<*comment* >

To insert a comment into the text (in Release 5 only):

  ^ONC<*comment* >**^KD**

or

  EDIT/Other/Footnote/endnote... /C
  <*comment* >

or

  EDIT/File/Save file, go to Opening screen

To view or edit a comment (in Release 5 only):

  ^OND

or

  EDIT/Other/Footnote/endnote... /D

| USAGE |

To insert a single-line comment, type **..** or **.IG** followed by the comment. The comment will not be displayed in preview mode or printed. Although you can see only 80 characters at a time because of the screen width, the comment can be as long as you like.

In Release 5 you can insert a comment into the text. To do so, type **^ONC**. A new window appears at the bottom of the screen. Type in the comment and then press **^KD** or use the equivalent command from either the File or the Window pull-down menu to close the window. If you have display set to on (**^OD**), a tag displays the first words of the comment in bright text or in a different color and enclosed in square brackets, like this:

[You left off he]

To view the entire comment or edit it, position the cursor on the comment tag and type **^OND**. You can then use the standard editing commands to modify the comment. To close the comment window without saving changes, press **^KQ**. To close the comment window and save changes, press **^KD**. You can also close the window using the equivalent commands on either the File or Window pull-down menu.

SEE ALSO

Notes

Copy

WordStar allows you to copy files and blocks of text.

RELEASE

4 and 5

KEY SEQUENCE

See individual sections.

USAGE

To copy a block of text into a new position or window, see
Block Operations: Copy Block. To copy single files within
WordStar, use the commands detailed in the following sections. To copy groups of files at one time, it is best to use the
DOS COPY or XCOPY commands with wild cards. Consult
your computer's DOS Reference Manual for details on these
commands.

Copying Files

KEY SEQUENCE

To copy a file from the Classic Opening menu:

O *<d:\pathname\file1>*
<d:\pathname\file2 >

To copy a file from the pull-down Opening menu in Release 5:

File/Copy a file.../*<d:\pathname\file1>*
<d:\pathname\file2 >

To copy a file from the Edit menu:

^KO*<d:\pathname\file1>*
<d:\pathname\file2 >

or (in Release 5 only):

EDIT/File/Copy a file.../*<d:\pathname\file1>*
<d:\pathname\file2 >

USAGE

To copy a file from the Opening menu, press **O** (or select
File/Copy a file...). You will see one of the following prompts:

Release 4:
Document to be copied?

Release 5:
File

Enter the name of the file you want to copy (including drive and path name, if necessary) and press ↵ or select the file from the directory display using **^X** and the cursor keys (or using arrow keys on numeric keypad) and then press ↵. You will then see the prompt

Release 4:
Name a document to hold the new copy.

Release 5:
Name of copy

Enter the name for the new file (including drive and path name if they are different from the logged drive and directory). WordStar will display a dot for every 4,000 characters it copies during the operation.

To copy files while editing a document, press **^KO** (or **EDIT/File/Copy a file...**). The rest of the procedure is the same as when the operation is performed from the Opening menu. However, if you copy the file you are working on (to save a backup copy with a different name or to a different drive, for instance), any changes made to the file since it was opened will not appear on the copy, unless you have saved using the **^KS** (or **F9**, or in Release 5 only, **EDIT/File/Save file, resume editing**) command. It will copy only the version of the file that you last saved.

In Release 5, you have the option of saving a file under a new name (**^KT**) and then returning to the original file. Use this option instead of **^KO** to make a copy of the file you are editing that includes all the editing changes you have made in that editing session but haven't yet saved.

SEE ALSO

Save

Cursor Movement

To move the cursor within your document, use the commands listed below.

RELEASE

4 and 5

KEY SEQUENCE

Basic cursor commands:

CURSOR MOVEMENT	COMMAND
Down one line	^X or ↓
Up one line	^E or ↑
Right one character	^D or →
Left one character	^S or ←
Down one screen	^C or PgDn
Up one screen	^R or PgUp
Right to next word	^F or ^→
Left to previous word	^A or ^←

Time-saving cursor commands:

CURSOR MOVEMENT	COMMAND
Left end of line	^QS or ^F9
Right end of line	^QD or ^F10
Top of screen	^QE or Home
Bottom of screen	^QX or End
Beginning of document	^QR or ^Home
End of document	^QC or ^End
Go to page* n	^QI n or ^F4 n [EDIT/Go to/Go to page.../n]
[Go n pages* back	^QI- n or ^F4- n or EDIT/Go to/Go to page.../- n]
[Go n pages* forward	^QI+ n or ^F4+ n or EDIT/Go to/Go to page.../+ n]
Go to beginning of block	^QB
Go to end of block	^QK

line(s) if in nondocument mode.
[ ] Release 5 only

USAGE

One of WordStar's fundamental advantages for the touch typist is the arrangement of the cursor control keys. While pressing the Ctrl key, you can move up a line, down a line, to the right or left by a character or a word, without ever having to look at the keyboard. The commands are centered around the "home key" touch typing position for the left hand. Commands to move up are above the home keys, those to move right are to the right of them, and so forth. If you are not a

touch typist, the cursor keypad can perform the same functions. NumLock must be turned off for these keys to function
properly, unless you have an extended keyboard that has
both a cursor and a numeric keypad.

Additional cursor movement commands are listed in the
Go To entry.

SEE ALSO

Go To

Scroll

Custom Print

In conjunction with dot commands, Release 4's customization program, WSCHANGE, and Release 5's printer customization program, PRCHANGE, Custom Print allows you
to select special codes to send to your printer.

RELEASE

4 and 5

KEY SEQUENCE

To insert a predefined special printer code into a document:

^PQ *or* **^PW** *or* **^PE** *or* **^PR**

To define a special printer code for a specific document (or override default settings for that code):

.XQ<*hexadecimal character codes* > *or*
.XW<*hexadecimal character codes* > *or*
.XE<*hexadecimal character codes* > *or*
.XR<*hexadecimal character codes* >

To define a special printer code one time (in Release 5 only):

^P! <*ASCII character code*>

or

^P! %x<*hexadecimal character code*>

USAGE	

WordStar provides you with so many print drivers that one of them will almost certainly work with your printer. But occasionally you will need to send your printer a specific code (to access a special font, or character, or change from portrait to landscape mode, to name three examples). For this reason, WordStar provides you with the means to have at least four preset printer codes that you can either program in WSCHANGE (Release 4), PRCHANGE (Release 5), or with dot commands at the beginning of a file. If you use dot commands, you are limited to a string of 24 *hexadecimal* character codes. (Hexadecimal is the base-16 numbering system often used in computers and printers, with numerals 0–9, then A–F.) Release 5 also has a custom print code that allows you to insert a print code into your document (**^P!**).

To set any of the four permanent print controls, first consult your print manual and locate the code sequence required to perform the desired function. If these are codes you will be using frequently, you should use WSCHANGE (Release 4) or PRCHANGE (Release 5) to install these codes as defaults. See Appendix A for information on the use of WSCHANGE and PRCHANGE. If you use custom printing only occasionally, or you are using a different printer temporarily, use the dot commands listed above to set the codes at the beginning of the document. To set the code for ^PQ, insert the commmand

.XQ *<hexadecimal character code>*

at the top of your document. At the location where you want the print control to take effect in your document, press ^PQ. The remaining three preset codes work identically.

Any codes preset with WSCHANGE or PRCHANGE will be overridden for any given with the dot command settings.

To insert a print code one time only in a document, press ^P! where you want the print control to take effect. The USER PRINT CONTROL dialog box appears. At the first option, Characters to send to the printer, you may either enter standard ASCII characters (alphanumeric and symbols) or hexadecimal characters. If you use ASCII characters, you must use the caret (^) to indicate the Ctrl character (do *not* press Ctrl). If you want a literal caret to be inserted, type %^. If you want an Esc code to be inserted, type ^[. To insert a % code, type %%. To use hexadecimal characters instead, begin the code sequence with %x. In the next option of the dialog box, specify any characters you wish to display when code display is off. The third option, Number of inches to account for on printer, can be used to tell WordStar the width of the inserted matter if it is to be printed (such as PostScript printer commands to produce graphics).

```
SEE ALSO
```

Print

Appendix A

Customizing WordStar

See **Appendix A**.

Date

The following commands allow you to insert the system date into your file.

RELEASE

4 and 5

KEY SEQUENCE

To insert the current system date as a text string in your document:

Esc-@

or (in Release 5 only):

EDIT/Other/Shorthand macros.../@

To insert a code to print the current system date at time of merge printing:

&@&

USAGE

In order for the date commands to function properly, you must set the DOS system date properly. If your computer is already set up with an internal clock that sets the system date when you turn your computer on, this step is not necessary. To set the date, exit from WordStar (although you can set the

date using the Run a DOS Command feature as well). At the
system prompt, type

C>DATE.⏎

Your system will display a message like

Current date is Mon   6-06-1989
Enter new date (mm-dd-yy):

If the date is correct, accept it by pressing ⏎. If not, enter the
correct date in the mm-dd-yy format requested.

To insert the date into the document, place your cursor
where you want the date to appear and press **Esc-@**. The date
will appear on the screen in the format month day, year. The
example above would appear as June 6, 1989. The date format can be changed using WSCHANGE. For more information, see Appendix A.

To print the current system date while merge printing, insert the code **&@&** at the place you want it to appear when
printing. The date format will be the same as with **Esc-@**.

SEE ALSO

Merge Print

Run a DOS Command

Time

Appendix A

Delete

The following commands allow you to remove documents
from your disk or sections of text from your document.

RELEASE

4 and 5

KEY SEQUENCE

See individual sections.

USAGE

To delete files, see the section **Deleting Files**. To delete blocks, see the entry **Block Operations: Delete Block**. To delete text, see **Deleting Text** below.

Deleting Files

The following commands allow you to delete files or groups of files in WordStar.

KEY SEQUENCE

To delete a file (or files) from the Classic Opening menu:

Y *<d:\pathname\filename.ext >*↵

To delete a file (or files) from the pull-down Opening menu:

File/Delete a file.../*<d:\pathname\filename.ext >* ↵

To delete a file (or files) from the Classic Edit menu:

^KJ *<d:\pathname\filename.ext >* ↵

To delete a file (or files) from the pull-down Opening menu:

EDIT/File/Delete a file.../*<d:\pathname\filename.ext >* ↵

To delete a single file from the Opening menu, press **Y** (or select **File/Delete a File** if you have Release 5 and are using pull-down menus). Next, enter the name of the file you wish to delete, or use the cursor movement keys to select a file from the current directory, and then press ↵. You can also specify a different drive or directory with the file name or use DOS wildcard characters (***** and **?**) to specify more than one file. Depending on your level setting, WordStar may display the message

Are you sure (Y/N)?

If you have selected the wrong file, this is your last chance to prevent its erasure—the Undo function does not work with file deletion. If you have selected the correct file or files, press **Y**.

If you have accidentally erased a file, DOS utility programs such as Norton Utilities and Mace Utilities can recover the erased data. If you have one of these utilities, remember that you should try to recover the file immediately because any disk activity (such as file-saving) runs the risk of overwriting your erased file.

To delete a file while editing another file, press **^KJ** (or also select **EDIT/File/Delete a File** in Release 5). Enter the name of the file as in the above procedure and press **Y**. This command is extremely useful if in the course of trying to save your current file, you discover that you are running out of disk space. You can delete a less important file (such as a backup file) to make more room.

As a safety measure, WordStar won't allow you to inadvertently delete the file you're currently working on. You must abandon the file (**^KQ**) or save it, and then delete it.

Deleting Text

The following commands can be used to delete sections of text. An asterisk next to the command means that the undo command (^U) will not restore text following that command.

TEXT TO DELETE	COMMAND
Character at cursor	^G or Del
Character preceding cursor	^H or Backspace
Word at and to right of cursor	^T or F6 [EDIT/Edit/Delete word]
Line	^Y or F5 [EDIT/Edit/Delete line]
Line to right of cursor	^QY
Line to left of cursor	^Q Del
From character to given character	^QT <char>
Sentence	^QT . (period)
Paragraph	^QT⏎
Marked block	^KY or Shift-F5 [EDIT/Edit/Delete block]

[ ] Release 5 only

The commands listed above delete the text designated. Word-Star saves in memory the last deletion longer than a character in length. For this reason, it is not only faster to use **^T** or **F6** to delete a word than to use **Del**, for instance, but also safer, since you can retrieve an accidental deletion from memory by pressing **^U** or **F2** (or EDIT/Edit/Undo in Release 5).

If you are deleting a section of text that is too large for Word-Star to unerase later, you will be prompted before the deletion is performed:

Release 4:
The block is too large to unerase later.
Erase anyway (Y/N)?

Release 5:
Too large to undo later. Delete anyway (Y/N)?

Answer yes if you're certain.

| SEE ALSO |

Block Operations: Delete Block

Undo

Directory

See **Drive.**

Directory Display

The following command turns the display of the current directory file listing on and off.

RELEASE

4 and 5

KEY SEQUENCE

To turn the display of files in the current directory on or off from the Classic Opening menu:

F

USAGE

To turn the display of the directory on or off, press **F** at the Opening menu. If you are using Release 5 pull-down menus, you cannot turn the display of directories off.

Document Mode

These commands allow you to open files in *document mode*, a file format that can include page and print formatting codes.

RELEASE

4 and 5

KEY SEQUENCE

To open a file in document mode from the Opening menu in Release 4:

D<*d:\pathname\filename.ext* >↵

To open and name a file or open an existing file in document mode from the Classic Opening menu in Release 5:

D<*d:\pathname\filename.ext* >↵

To open a new document file from the Classic Opening menu in Release 5 in document mode without naming it first:

S

To open and name a file or open an existing file in document mode from the pull-down Opening menu in Release 5:

File/Open a document file...
<*d:\pathname\filename.ext* >↵

To open a new document file from the pull-down Opening menu in Release 5 in document mode without naming it first (unless you have changed the default mode to nondocument, in which case a nondocument file is opened):

File/Speed Write (new file)/
<*d:\pathname\filename.ext* >↵

To open and name a file or open an existing file in document mode from the DOS prompt:

D>WS <*d:\pathname\filename.ext* >↵

or, if you have changed the default mode to nondocument in Release 4:

D>WS <*d:\pathname\filename.ext* >↵ **D**

or, if you have changed the default mode to nondocument in Release 5:

D>WS <*d:\pathname\filename.ext* >⏎ /D

USAGE ══════════════════════════

WordStar has two file formats, *document mode* and *nondocument mode*. Document mode is the standard file format; it inserts codes for page and print formatting and enhancements. Most printed documents are best produced in document mode. Nondocument mode, without these codes, is primarily used for command files and plain ASCII text files (to be used with programming language compilers, or read by another word processing program).

To open an existing document file from the Classic Opening menu in Release 4 or Release 5, press **D** and type in the name of the file (including drive and directory if different from the current one). You can also select a file by pressing **^X** or ↓ to move from the prompt line to the directory (if it is displayed) and then using the cursor keys to select the appropriate file. When the cursor is on the correct file, press ⏎.

To open and name a new document file from the Classic Opening menu in Release 4 or Release 5, press **D** as above and type in the new file name. You will see the following prompt (unless you are using Release 4 with help level 0 or 1):

Can't find that file. Create a new one (Y/N)?

Answer **Y** and a new file will be opened.

To open a new document file to be named later (an option available in Release 5 only) press **S** from the Classic Opening menu, or select **File/Speed Write (new file)** if you are using the pull-down menu interface. After typing the document, you will be prompted to assign it a name when you try to save it or close the document.

SEE ALSO

Nondocument Mode
Open a Document
Save
Speed Write

DOS

See **Run a DOS Command.**

Dot Commands

RELEASE

4 and 5

KEY SEQUENCE

To insert a dot command:

.AA

where AA is any dot command.
To insert a dot command with values:

.AA *<numeric variable, ON/OFF, or text string >*

where AA is any dot command.

USAGE

Dot commands are used to insert instructions into an individual file. They are used in nearly every aspect of the program. Individual dot commands are described throughout the Topical Reference section.

To insert a dot command into a file, position the cursor at the left margin (column 1). Type a period (.) immediately followed by the desired dot command, with no space between the period and the dot command. (Dot commands are printed uppercase in this book, but WordStar will also recognize either upper- or lowercase letters.) If the dot command also has a value, such as a number or text string, it can be separated from the dot command by a space for ease of reading. Finally, the dot command or dot command and value must be followed by a hard carriage return (↵).

The flag column (the rightmost column on the screen) will display information (flags) regarding the dot command. The following list shows the meaning of the flags that relate specifically to dot commands.

?   Unrecognized (invalid) dot command

+   Line extends past rightmost column of screen

1   Dot command changes printed page and screen appearance; should be at beginning of file

.   Dot command changes printed page and screen

:   Dot command changes printed page only

In Release 5, making selections within a dialog box or through the pull-down menus often automatically inserts the correct dot command sequence that corresponds to the desired action when the command is executed or the options in the dialog box are accepted.

If you are using a complex set of dot commands and want to see them in print, print the document in nondocument mode. You can suppress the display of dot commands by using Page Preview (**^OP**).

Dot Leaders

This command inserts dot leaders in the space between two sections of text.

RELEASE

5 only

KEY SEQUENCE

^P.

USAGE

This feature is useful for inserting a row of dots between items and numbers, as in a table of contents or a price list. To insert dot leaders, position the cursor immediately following the last character of the item in the list or table and then press ^P. repeatedly until you reach your desired column of numbers. The command operates like the Tab key and inserts dots instead of spaces as it moves the cursor to the next tab stop to the right.

Double Strike

This command causes certain printers to strike printed characters twice to make them appear bolder.

RELEASE

4 and 5

KEY SEQUENCE

^PD<*text* >**^PD**

USAGE

Double strike text is useful with certain impact printers (daisy-wheel and dot-matrix printers) to produce slightly bolder text. The command causes each character to be struck (printed) twice in the same place. This command can also be useful if you have a printer ribbon that is starting to become faint. Double strike is distinguished from boldface in that it prints only twice, whereas boldface prints each character three times on impact printers.

To initiate double strike type in your document, use the **^PD** command. To turn double strike off, simply press **^PD** once more; it operates as a toggle key. If you have WordStar set to display print control characters, you will see the text you coded for double strike appear as shown:

This is a sample of text **^Dwith double strike added.**^D

Note that the double strike text will appear brighter or in a different color on your screen. If you turn print control display off, this text will remain highlighted, but without the ^D symbols.

Boldface

Drive

These commands allow you to change the drive and directory in which you are working.

4 and 5

To change the drive or directory in Release 4 or Release 5, from the Classic Opening menu:

L *<d:\directory >*

where *d* is the drive letter.

To change the drive or directory in Release 5 from the Opening menu using pull-down menus:

File/Change drive/directory... *<d:\directory >*

where *d* is the drive letter.

To change the drive or directory in either Release while editing a document:

^KL <*d:\directory* >

where *d* is the drive letter.

To change the drive or directory in Release 5 using pull-down menus while editing a document:

EDIT/File/Change drive/directory...<*d:\directory* >

where *d* is the drive letter.

USAGE

To change the default drive or directory (to change the *logged* disk drive or directory) from the Opening menu, select the appropriate key sequence listed above.

If you have Release 4, a screen will appear with instructions, a list of available disk drives, the name of the current drive and directory, and a display of the files and subdirectories in the current directory. The subdirectories will appear preceded by a backslash to distinguish them from file names:

\ LETTERS
\ INVOICES

To select a subdirectory of the current directory, you can either type the name and press ↵ or press ^X or ↓ to move the cursor into the directory listing and then, using the cursor movement keys, select the appropriate subdirectory and press ↵. To select a new drive or a directory that is not a subdirectory of the current one, you must type in the new name. You cannot create a new directory in this manner; you must use the DOS MKDIR (or MD) command, either from the DOS prompt after exiting WordStar or with the Run a DOS Command feature in WordStar. See your DOS technical reference manual for more details.

If you have Release 5, a dialog box will appear displaying a list of available disk drives, with the name of the current drive and directory on the prompt line and a display of the files and subdirectories in the current directory below it. The subdirectories will appear followed by a backslash to distinguish them from file names:

LETTERS   \
INVOICES   \

To select a subdirectory of the current directory, you can either edit the current drive and directory name and press ⏎ or press ^X or ↓ to move the cursor into the directory listing and then, using the cursor movement keys, select the appropriate subdirectory and press ⏎. If you want to select a new drive or a directory that is not a subdirectory of the current one, you must type in the new name. You cannot create a new directory in this manner; you must use the DOS MKDIR (or MD) command, either from the DOS prompt after exiting WordStar or with the Run a DOS Command feature in WordStar. See your DOS technical reference manual for more details.

To change the default drive or directory while editing a file, select the appropriate key sequence listed above. This command functions the same as the equivalent command from the Opening menu.

To change the default drive and directory names in which WordStar's program files are located, use WSCHANGE. See Appendix A for details.

NOTE

If you change directories while editing a document, the document will *not* be saved in the new logged drive or directory, but in the one in which it was first opened.

SEE ALSO

Run a DOS Command

Appendix A

Endnotes

See **Notes.**

Erase

See **Delete.**

Esc

See **Shorthand.**

Exit

The following commands allow you to leave WordStar and return to DOS.

RELEASE

4 and 5

KEY SEQUENCE

See individual sections.

USAGE

The two ways to exit WordStar properly are both described below. *Never* leave WordStar by simply turning your computer off. If you do, any document that you are working on will be destroyed, and you may also damage your disks.

Exiting WordStar from the Opening Menu

The following commands allow you to exit WordStar from the Opening menu.

KEY SEQUENCE

To exit from from the Classic Opening menu:

X

To exit from Release 5 using the pull-down menus:

File/Exit WordStar

USAGE

To exit from WordStar to the operating system at the Classic Opening menu, simply press **X** (or **File/Exit WordStar** if you are using Release 5 pull-down menus). If you are printing or merge printing a file, WordStar will not let you exit unless you allow the file to finish printing or abandon the printing session by pressing **P** and then **^U** on the Printing menu.

Exiting WordStar from within a File

The following commands allow you to save the current file, exit WordStar, and return to DOS.

KEY SEQUENCE

To exit WordStar and save the current file from Release 4 or Release 5 from the Classic Opening menu:

^KX

To exit WordStar and save the current file from Release 5 using the pull-down menus:

EDIT/File/Save file, exit WordStar

USAGE

To exit from WordStar to the operating system and save the file you have been working on, press **^KX** (or select **EDIT/File/Save file, exit WordStar** if you are using Release 5 pull-down menus). If you don't want to save your current file, press **^KQ** to abandon your edit—answering **Y** when Word-Star asks if you're sure—and then press **X** from the Opening menu (or select File/Exit WordStar using pull-down menus).

Extended Character Set

See **Graphics Characters.**

File Management

See **Copy, Delete, Drive, Protect/Unprotect, Rename, Save.**

Find

See **Go To.**

Fixed Position

See **Column Alignment.**

Fonts

See **Choose Font.**

Footers

The following commands allow you to place *footers*—lines of text that appear at the bottom of each page—in your document and adjust their position on the page.

RELEASE

4 and 5

KEY SEQUENCE

See individual sections.

USAGE

Footers can be used to print up to three lines of repeating information about the document at the bottom of each page. Codes can be inserted to print different text on odd- and even-numbered pages and print page numbers in the footers. The location of the footers on the page can also be adjusted. Since the commands differ slightly between Releases 4 and 5, see the sections that correspond to your version of the program.

Inserting Footers (Release 4 Only)

KEY SEQUENCE

To insert a single line footer or the first line of a multiline footer:

.FO<text >

or

  .F1<*text* >

To insert a second line footer:

  .F2<*text* >

To insert a third line footer:

  .F3<*text* >

To print footers on alternating sides of pages:

  .FO   <*text* >

| USAGE |

To place a one-line footer into your document, insert the dot command **.FO** or **.F1** somewhere before the end of the first page (although for consistency's sake inserting the command at the beginning of the page is preferable), followed by a space (optional) and then the footer text, which can be up to 100 characters in length per line. Characters include carriage returns and codes. If you use extended (graphics) characters not on the keyboard, each one counts as three characters. If you require longer footers, you can extend the number of characters possible with WSCHANGE (see Appendix A). The character width and font will be those active before you inserted the footer command. To change the font or character width of a footer, place the appropriate dot commands immediately preceding the footer command. You can use any of the standard print control commands—such as boldface—within the footer, although they will not be highlighted on the screen; you must have codes set to display with **^OD** or **Shift-F1** to see the command codes. Be sure to reset any formatting codes after the footer command to their original settings.

   To add a second or second and third line to the footer, simply use the **.F2** and **.F3** commands accompanied by text. If you want to insert a blank line between two lines in the footer, insert the first footer line, press ↵, and then type **.F2** followed by *two* spaces, press ↵, and then type **.F3** followed by the third footer line. If you use only one space after **.F2**, WordStar will ignore the command because it ignores the first space immediately following all dot commands.

You can also put the current page number in as part of the footer by placing the pound symbol (#) where you want the page number to appear. It is not necessary to turn off page numbering; WordStar will automatically disable other page number placement commands and print the page number in the footer. If you want to use the pound symbol in your text but not as a page number marker, type a backslash before the pound symbol, like this: \#. Only the pound symbol will be printed. If you want to use a backslash in your footer, type two backslashes (\\); one will be printed.

Sometimes it is desirable to have a footer print on the outside margin of each page, as is done in some books. To do this, insert the footer command and then press **^PK**. Then press the Spacebar or the Tab key until you have reached the column at which you want the right-hand (odd) page footer to appear on the page. Now type the footer text and then press ↵. What the ^PK command actually does is take out those spaces you inserted to the right of it on every *even* page, so that on left-hand (even) pages, the footer is printed at the left margin, and on right-hand pages it is printed at the right. If you want the right-hand page footer to be flush with the right margin, make sure that the last letter of the footer text is at the last column before the right margin in the footer dot command.

To turn footers off in a document, insert a footer code with no spaces or text following it for each code you inserted. For example, if you want to turn off a three-line footer, type the following:

.F1
.F2
.F3

Footer Margins (Release 4 Only)

This command allows you to adjust the number of blank lines separating the footer from the text.

KEY SEQUENCE

.FM *n*

where *n* is the number of lines separating the first line of the footer from the last line of text.

USAGE

The margin between footer and text is normally two blank lines. To decrease the footer margin to one blank line, insert the command **.FM1** below the footer command. To have no blank line separating text and footer, insert the command **.FM0**. To insert more than two blank lines, you must consider the bottom page margin and your page length to make sure the footers print properly. Since the footer is considered part of the bottom page margin, and the default bottom margin is eight lines, the footer margin plus the number of lines in the footer cannot exceed eight unless you change the size of the bottom margin. The calculation of the number of lines is relative to the line height setting. If you change the line height, you must take this into account when calculating your margins.

Inserting Footers (Release 5 Only)

KEY SEQUENCE

To insert a single line footer or the first line of a multiline footer:

.FO*<text >*

or

.F1<*text*>

or

EDIT/Layout/Footer...<*text*>

To insert a second line footer:

.F2<*text*>

To insert a third line footer:

.F3<*text*>

To print footers on even-numbered pages:

.FOe<*text*>

To print footers on odd-numbered pages:

.FOo<*text*>

USAGE

To place a one-line footer into your document, insert the dot command **.FO** or **.F1** somewhere before the end of the first page (although for consistency's sake inserting the command at the beginning of the page is preferable), followed by a space (optional) and then the footer text, which can be up to 100 characters in length per line. Characters include carriage returns and codes. If you use extended (graphics) characters not on the keyboard, each one counts as three characters. If you require longer footers, you can extend the number of characters possible with WSCHANGE (see Appendix A). The character width and font will be those active before you inserted the footer command. To change the font or character width of a footer, place the appropriate dot commands immediately preceding the footer command, or place the font tags within the footer text and then return the font and character width settings to their previous values afterwards. You can use any of the standard print control commands—such as

boldface—within the footer, although they will not be highlighted on the screen; you must have codes set to display with
^OD or **Shift-F1** to see the command codes.

To add a second or second and third line to the footer, simply use the **.F2** and **.F3** commands accompanied by text. To insert a blank line between two lines in the footer, insert the first
footer line, press ↵, type **.F2** followed by *two* spaces, press ↵,
and then type **.F3** followed by the third footer line. If you use
only one space after **.F2**, WordStar will ignore the command
because it ignores the first space immediately following all
dot commands.

You can also put the current page number in as part of the
footer by placing the pound symbol (#) where you want
the page number to appear. It is not necessary to turn off page
numbering; WordStar will automatically disable other page
numbering commands automatically and print the page
number in the footer. If you want to use the pound symbol in
your text but not as a page number marker, type a backslash
before the pound symbol, like this: \#. Only the pound symbol will be printed. If you want to use a backslash in your
footer, type two backslashes (\\); one will be printed.

To insert different footers for odd- and even-numbered
pages, type an **e** for even pages immediately after the dot
command as shown in the key sequence above, or an **o** for
odd pages. If you want to have alternate footers that are flush
with the outside margin, use the Spacebar or Tab key to make
sure that the odd-numbered (that is, right-hand) footer text
ends at the last column before the right margin of the page.
(The ^PK command from previous releases of WordStar no
longer functions; the odd/even feature is meant to take its
place.)

To turn footers off in a document, insert a footer code with
no spaces or text following it for each code you inserted. For
example, if you want to turn off a three-line footer, type the
following:

.F1
.F2
.F3

Footer Margins (Release 5 Only)

This command allows you to adjust the amount of space separating the footer from the text.

To change the footer margin using inches as the unit of measurement:

.FM *n.nn*"

or

^OL
Footer
n.nn
^K [*or* **F10**]

or

Edit/Layout/Margins and tabs.../Footer/*n.nn*
^K [*or* **F10**]

where *n.nn* is the number of inches separating the first line of the footer from the last line of text.

To change the footer margin using lines as the unit of measurement:

.FM *n*

where *n* is the number of lines separating the first line of the footer from the last line of text.

Either inches or lines can be used as a unit of measurement when setting the footer margin. Using either ^OL or the EDIT/Layout pull-down menu will first bring you to the MARGINS & TABS dialog box. Tab down six times to the Footer setting and type the desired number in inches for the footer margin. It will automatically be inserted as a dot command in inches. Once you have made the necessary changes, press ^K or **F10** to exit the dialog box.

You can insert the footer margin as a dot command directly by typing **.FM** followed by the margin size in lines or inches. This way, the header and bottom margins will not be reset automatically with it. If you do not use an inch symbol ("), WordStar assumes the measurement is in lines.

The margin between footer and text is normally two blank lines, or .33 in. To decrease the footer margin to one blank line, insert the command **.FM1** or **.FM .17"** below the footer command. To have no blank line separating text and footer, insert the command **.FM0** or **.FM 0"**. To insert more than two blank lines, you must take into consideration the bottom page margin and your page length to make sure the footers print properly. Since the footer is considered part of the bottom page margin, and the default bottom margin is eight lines or 1.33 in., the footer margin plus the number of lines in the footer cannot exceed eight lines or 1.33 in. unless you change the size of the bottom margin. The calculation using the number of lines is relative to the line height setting. If you change the line height, you must take this change into account as well when calculating your margins.

SEE ALSO

Headers

Line Height

Margins

Page Numbering

Footnotes

See **Notes.**

Form Feed

These commands cause your printer to advance to the next page from anywhere in the line and specify custom form feed strings for printers.

RELEASE

4 and 5

KEY SEQUENCE

To insert a form feed:

^PL

To specify a custom form feed string for the printer:

.XL<*form feed code for your printer* >

USAGE

To cause your printer to advance to the next page from within a line of text, use the form feed command **^PL**. You'll see ^L and a line across the remainder of the screen (as with a standard page break) and an **F** in the flag column. Form feed operates similarly to the page-break dot command (.PA), but can be used without inserting a dot command on a separate line. It will function properly only if your printer understands form feeds.

If your printer needs a custom command string to cause a form feed (other than the one provided for that printer driver), you can specify this string with the dot command **.XL** followed by the required string. The dot command must appear before the first ^PL code for the form feed feature to function properly.

SEE ALSO

Page Break

Function Key Display

See **Appendix A.**

Function Keys

See **inside front cover.**

Go To

The following commands allow you to locate a specific string of text, position, or code in your text.

RELEASE

4 and 5

KEY SEQUENCE

See individual sections.

USAGE

WordStar has a great number of commands for locating specific items within a document. To find a specific string of text, see the subsections **Find (Release 4 Only)** and **Find (Release 5 Only)**. To locate a specific relative position (such as page 4) or a code or tag, see the subsections **Go To Commands (Release 4 Only)** or **Go To Commands (Release 5 Only)**. To find and replace text, see **Replace** later in the Topical Reference section.

Find (Release 4 Only)

The following commands find a specified text string within a document.

KEY SEQUENCE

To search for a specific text string:

^QF<*text* >⏎
<*options* >⏎

or

Ctrl-F1 <*text* >⏎
<*options* >⏎

To repeat the last search:

^L

or

Ctrl-F3

USAGE

To find a specific string of text within a document, press **^QF**. Type in the string of characters you want to find. If you are looking for something similar to what you sought in a previous search, pressing **^R** will insert the string of characters from the last ^QF or ^QA (Replace) operation. You can use the normal editing keys to change or delete characters. To search for codes that appear in the text, you must press **^P** before the control code in order for it to be understood. For instance, to find boldface codes, you must press **^P^B**, not just **^B**. To find a hard carriage return (usually the end of a paragraph), press **^N**; the code **^M^J** appears in the search string, indicating a hard return. You can use the question mark (?) as a wild-card character to represent any character if you later select the wild-card option. For instance, to search for all five-letter words beginning with *qu*, you would type **qu???** as your text string. The text string to search for can be up to 65 characters long (including codes). When you are finished typing it, press ⏎ and the cursor moves down to the Options prompt.

At the Options prompt, you can specify certain aspects of how the search will be performed. Options can be combined in any logical combination. To enter an option, simply press the corresponding letter at the prompt. If you select more than one, type them consecutively in any order but with no spaces between them. The following is a list of options available and a description of their functions.

CODE   FUNCTION

B   Searches backward through the text toward the beginning of the document from the current cursor position.

G   Searches from the beginning (or end if B is also selected) of the document.

U   Searches for either uppercase or lowercase occurrences of the characters in the text string.

W   Searches for whole words only.

?   Treats ? characters in the search string as wildcard characters instead of literal question marks.

n   Searches for the *n*th occurrence of the search string.

If you want to repeat a search for the string you last specified, simply press **^L**. This command will repeat either the last Find or Replace operation; if you performed a Replace operation last, you must press **^QF ^R ↵ ^R ↵** instead to repeat a Find operation. Also note that the Repeat Search command does not allow you to change options.

Go To Commands (Release 4 Only)

The following commands take you to a specific place in a document.

COMMAND	FUNCTION
^Q0–^Q9	Goes to place marker of that number.
^QB	Goes to beginning of block.
^QC *or* Ctrl-End	Goes to end of file.
^QD *or* Ctrl-F10	Goes to end of line.
^QG*x*	Goes to next occurrence of character *x*.
^QG.⏎	Goes to end of paragraph.
^QG.	Goes to end of sentence ending in period.
^QH*x*	Goes backward to last occurrence of character *x*.
^QI *n or* Ctrl-F4 *n*	Goes to page *n* (in document mode) or line *n* (in nondocument mode).
^QK	Goes to end of block.
^QP	Goes to cursor location before last command.
^QR *or* Ctrl-Home	Goes to beginning of file.
^QS *or* Ctrl-F9	Goes to beginning of line.
^QV	Goes to last find or block, whether visible or not.

USAGE

These commands can greatly increase the speed of moving around within the text.

Cursor Movement

Place Markers

Replace

Find (Release 5 Only)

The following commands find a specified text string within a document.

KEY SEQUENCE

To search for a specific text string:

^QF<text >↵
<options >↵

or

Ctrl-F1 <text >↵
<options >↵

or

EDIT/Go to/Find text.../<text >↵
<options >↵

To repeat the last search:

^L

or

Ctrl-F3

or

EDIT/Go to/Repeat previous find/replace

| **USAGE** |

To find a specific string of text within a document, press **^QF** or select **Find text...** from the EDIT/Go to menu. Type in the string of characters you want to find. The last text string will already appear in the dialog box. You can use the normal editing keys to change or delete characters. To search for codes that appear in the text, you must press **^P** before the control code in order for it to be understood. For instance, to find boldface codes, you must press **^P^B**, not just **^B**. To find a hard carriage return (usually the end of a paragraph), enter the code **^N**, which will appear as **^P^M^P^J**. To search for font tags or notes, see the following section, **Go To Commands (Release 5 Only)**. You can use the question mark **(?)** as a wild-card character to represent any character if you later select the wild-card option. For instance, if you want to search for all five-letter words beginning with *qu*, you would type **qu???** as your text string. The text string to search for can be up to 65 characters long (including codes). When you are finished typing it, press ↵ and the cursor moves down to the Options prompt.

At the Options prompt, you can specify certain aspects of how the search will be performed. Options can be combined in any logical combination. To enter an option, simply press the corresponding letter at the prompt. If you select more than one, type them consecutively in any order. The following is a list of options available and a description of their functions.

CODE	FUNCTION
B	Searches backward through the text toward the beginning of the document from the current cursor position.
G	Searches from the beginning (or end if B is also selected) of the document.
U	Searches for either uppercase or lowercase occurrences of the characters in the text string.
W	Searches for whole words only.

? Treats ? characters in the search string as wild-card characters instead of as literal question marks.

n Searches for the *n*th occurrence of the search string.

If you want to repeat a search for the string you last specified, simply press ^L. This command will repeat either the last Find or Replace operation; if you performed a Replace operation last, you must press ^QF ^R ↵ ^R ↵ instead to repeat a Find operation. Also note that the Repeat Search command does not allow you to change options.

Go To Commands (Release 5 Only)

The following commands take you to a specific place in a document.

KEY SEQUENCE

To go to a specific place marker numbered 0–9:

^Q0–^Q9

To go to the beginning of the block:

^QB

or

EDIT/Go to/Go to block beginning

To go to the end of the file:

^QC

or

Ctrl-End

or

EDIT/Go to/Go to file end

To go to the end of the line:

^QD

or

Ctrl-F10

or

EDIT/Go to/Go to line end

To go to the next occurrence of character x:

^QG x

To go to the end of the paragraph:

^QG⌐

or

EDIT/Go to/Go to paragraph end

To go backward to the last occurrence of character x:

^QH x

To go to page n (in document mode) or line n (in nondocument mode):

^QI n

or

Ctrl-F4 n

or

EDIT/Go to/Go to page.../n

To go to the end of the block:

^QK

or

EDIT/Go to/Go to block end

To go to the cursor location before the last command:

^QP

To go to the beginning of the file:

^QR

or

Ctrl-Home

or

EDIT/Go to/Go to file beginning

To go to the beginning of the line:

^QS

or

Ctrl-F9

or

EDIT/Go to/Go to line beginning

To go to last find or block, whether that block is hidden or visible (marked):

^QV

To go to the next font:

^Q=

or

EDIT/Go to/Go to next font

To go to the next note:

^ONG

or

EDIT/Other/Footnote/endnote.../G

USAGE

These commands can greatly increase the speed of moving around within the text.

SEE ALSO

Cursor Movement

Place Markers

Replace

Graphics Characters

The following commands allow you to insert characters not on your keyboard into your file.

RELEASE

4 and 5

KEY SEQUENCE

To draw graphic border characters (also called "line" or "box" characters):

COMMAND   GRAPHIC CHARACTER

Alt-F1 |

Alt-F2   —

Alt-F3   ⌐

Alt-F4   ¬

Alt-F5   └

Alt-F6   ┘

Alt-F7   ┬

Alt-F8   ┴

Alt-F9   ├

Alt-F10   ┤

To draw ASCII extended graphic characters:

Alt<0–255 on numeric keypad >

To display and then select ASCII extended graphic characters
(Release 5 only):

^P0<0–255 >⌐

USAGE ══════════════════════════

WordStar has assigned the ten function keys in combination
with Alt to the border- or box-drawing characters of the IBM
extended character set. Press **Alt** and the appropriate function key to insert the character into your file. Although it will
be displayed on your screen, it might not be possible to print
out. Only graphics printers such as dot-matrix and laser
printers can produce characters like those you see on the
screen and then only if they have fonts with those characters.
Consult the documentation for your printer to ascertain its
capabilities and limits.

   To insert an extended graphic character other than those
assigned to function keys, such as a black square to be used
as a bullet or a shading character to be used in a bar graph,
press **Alt** and hold it down while you press the corresponding number on the numeric keypad. (Do not use the number
keys on the top row of the keyboard.) When you release your

finger from the Alt key, the character will appear on the screen. For example, to insert a British pound symbol into your document (£), press **Alt-156**.

If you have Release 5, you can press **^P0** to view the possible characters and then type the corresponding number and press ↵. The character will be inserted into your document.

Graphics Tag

This command allows you to insert a graphic file into your document at print time using the program Inset.

RELEASE

5 only

KEY SEQUENCE

^P*<d:\pathname\filename.ext >*

USAGE

To insert a graphics tag for the Inset graphics program (not included with WordStar) press **^P*** where you want Inset to insert the graphic image within your page, followed by the file name of that graphic image. Note that the graphic image will not be displayed in Page Preview, only on your printout. For more information, see your Inset documentation.

Hard Return Conversion

In document mode, this command converts hard returns (line breaks initiated by pressing the ↵ key) to soft returns (those inserted automatically by WordStar with word wrap).

VERSION

4 and 5

KEY SEQUENCE

In document mode only:

   ^6

USAGE

To convert hard returns to soft returns, position the cursor on the line ending in a hard return (marked with a < symbol in the flag column) and press ^6. The < symbol will disappear. Press ^B or ^QU to realign the paragraph. This command is useful for making word wrap function properly when you have received a text file from another word processing program with hard returns on every line.

Headers

The following commands allow you to place *headers*—lines of text that appear within the top margin at the top of each page—in your document and adjust their position.

RELEASE

4 and 5

KEY SEQUENCE

See individual sections.

USAGE

Headers can be used to print up to three lines of repeating information about the document at the top of each page. Codes can be inserted to print different text on odd- and even-numbered pages and print page numbers in the headers. The location of the headers on the page can also be adjusted. Since the commands differ slightly between Releases 4 and 5, see the sections that correspond to your version of the program.

Inserting Headers (Release 4 Only)

KEY SEQUENCE

To insert a single line header or the first line of a multiline header:

.HE *<text>*

or

.H1 *<text>*

To insert a second line header:

.H2 *<text>*

To insert a third line header:

.H3 *<text>*

To print headers on alternating sides of pages:

.HE^PK   *<text>*

USAGE

To place a one-line header into your document, insert the dot command **.HE** or **.H1** at the top of the page (before any text or blank lines) followed by a space (optional) and then the header text, which can be up to 100 characters in length per line. Characters include carriage returns and codes. If you use extended (graphics) characters not on the keyboard, each one counts as three characters. If you require longer headers, you can extend the number of characters possible with WSCHANGE (see Appendix A). The character width and font will be those active before you inserted the header command. To change the font or character width of a header, place the appropriate dot commands immediately preceding the header command. You can use any of the standard print control commands—such as boldface—within the header, although they will not be highlighted on the screen; you must have codes set to display with **^OD** or **Shift-F1** to see the command codes.

To add a second or second and third line to the header, simply use the **.H2** and **.H3** commands accompanied by text. If you want to insert a blank line between two lines in the header, insert the first header line, press ↵, type **.H2** followed by *two* spaces, press ↵, and then type **.H3** followed by the third header line. If you use only one space after **.H2**, Word-Star will ignore the command because it ignores the space immediately following all dot commands.

You can also put the current page number in as part of the header by placing the pound symbol (#) where you want the page number to appear. If you want to use the pound symbol in your text but not as a page number marker, type a backslash before the pound symbol, like this: \#. Only the pound symbol will be printed. If you want to use a backslash in your header, type two backslashes (\\); one will be printed.

Sometimes it is desirable to have a header print on the outside margin of each page, as is done in some books. To do this, press **^PK** and then insert the header command; next, press the Spacebar until you have reached the column at which you want the right-hand (odd) page header to appear on the page. Now type the header text and then press ↵. What the ^PK command actually does is take out those spaces you inserted to the right of it on every *even* page, so that on left-hand (even) pages, the header is printed at the left margin, and on right-hand pages it is printed to the right. If you want the right-hand page header to be flush with the right margin, make sure that the last letter of the header text is at the column before the right margin in the header dot command.

To turn headers off in a document, insert a header code with no spaces or text following it for each code you inserted. For example, if you want to turn off a three-line header, type the following:

    .H1
    .H2
    .H3

To print the first page without a header (if you use letterhead for your cover sheet and plain paper for the rest of your document, for instance), insert a blank line (using either ↵ or **^N**) above the first line of the header; it will not print until the following page.

Header Margins (Release 4 Only)

This command allows you to adjust the amount of space separating the header from the text.

KEY SEQUENCE

.HM *n*

where *n* is the number of lines separating the last line of the header from the first line of text.

USAGE

The margin between a one-line header and text is normally two blank lines. To decrease the header margin to one blank line separating text and header, insert the command **.HM1**. To have no blank lines between the header and the text, insert the command **.HM0**. To insert more than two blank lines, you must consider the top page margin and page length to make sure the headers print properly. Since the header is considered part of the top page margin, and the default top margin is three lines, the header margin plus the number of lines in the header cannot exceed three unless you change the size of the top margin. The calculation of the number of lines is relative to the line height setting. If you change the line height, you must take this change into account when calculating your margins.

Inserting Headers (Release 5 Only)

KEY SEQUENCE

To insert a single line header or the first line of a multiline header:

.HE *<text >*

or

.H1 *<text>*

or

EDIT/Layout/Header...*<text>*

To insert a second line header:

.H2 *<text>*

To insert a third line header:

.H3 *<text>*

To print headers on even-numbered pages:

.HEe *<text>*

To print headers on odd-numbered pages:

.HEo *<text>*

USAGE

To place a one-line header into your document, insert the dot command **.HE** or **.H1** at the top of the first page, followed by a space (optional) and then the header text, which can be up to 100 characters in length per line. Characters include carriage returns and codes. If you use extended (graphics) characters not on the keyboard, each one counts as three characters. If you require longer headers, you can extend the number of characters possible with WSCHANGE (see Appendix A). The character width and font will be those active before you inserted the header command. To change the font or character width of a header, place the appropriate dot commands immediately preceding the header command, or place the font tags within the header text. You can use any of the standard print control commands—such as boldface—within the header, although they will not be highlighted on the screen; you must have codes set to display with **^OD** or **Shift-F1** to see the command codes.

To add a second or second and third line to the header, simply use the **.H2** and **.H3** commands accompanied by text. If you want to insert a blank line between two lines in the header, insert the first header line, press ⏎, and then type **.H2** followed by *two* spaces, press ⏎, and then type **.H3** followed by the third header line. If you use only one space after **.H2**, WordStar will ignore the command because it ignores the space immediately following all dot commands.

You can also put the current page number in as part of the header by placing the pound symbol (#) where you want the page number to appear. If you want to use the pound symbol in your text but not as a page number marker, type a backslash before the pound symbol, like this: \#. Only the pound symbol will be printed. If you want to use a backslash in your header, type two backslashes (\\); one will be printed.

To insert different headers for odd- and even-numbered pages, type an **e** for even pages immediately after the dot command as shown in the key sequence above, or an **o** for odd pages. If you want to have alternate headers that are flush with the outside margin, use the Spacebar or Tab key to make sure that the odd-numbered (that is, right-hand) header text ends at the last column before the right margin of the page. (The ^PK command from previous releases of WordStar no longer functions; the odd/even feature is meant to take its place.)

To turn headers off in a document, insert a header code with no spaces or text following it for each code you inserted. For example, if you want to turn off a three-line header, type the following:

.H1
.H2
.H3

To print the first page without a header (if you use letterhead for your cover sheet and plain paper for the rest of your document, for instance), insert a blank line (using either ⏎ or **^N**) above the first line of the header; it will not print until the following page.

Header Margins (Release 5 Only)

This command allows you to adjust the amount of space separating the header from the text.

KEY SEQUENCE

To change the header margin using inches as the unit of measurement:

.HM *n.nn"*

or

^OL
Header
n.nn
^K [*or* **F10**]

or

EDIT/Layout/Margins and tabs.../Header/*n.nn*
^K [*or* **F10**]

where *n.nn* is the number of inches separating the last line of the header from the first line of text.

To change the header margin using lines as the unit of measurement:

.HM *n*

where *n* is the number of lines separating the last line of the header from the first line of text.

USAGE

Either inches or lines can be used as a unit of measurement when setting the header margin. If you use ^OL or the

EDIT/Layout pull-down menu, you will first access the MAR-
GINS & TABS dialog box. Tab down five times to the Header setting and type the desired number in inches for the header
margin. It will automatically be inserted as a dot command in
inches. Using this method, it is best to set the bottom and footer
margins (if necessary) because they will be inserted into the text
as dot commands, with whatever values appear in the dialog
box along with the header margin, when you exit the MAR-
GINS & TABS dialog box. Once you have made the necessary
changes, press **^K** or **F10** to exit the dialog box.

You can insert the header margin as a dot command directly by typing **.HM** followed by the margin size in lines or inches. This way, the footer and bottom margins will not be
reset automatically with it. If you do not use an inch symbol
("), WordStar assumes that measurement is in lines.

The margin between a one-line header and text is normally two blank lines, or .33 in. To decrease the header margin to
one blank line, insert the command **.HM1** or **.HM .17"** below
the header command. To have no blank line separating text
and header, insert the command **.HM0** or **.HM 0"**. To insert
more than two blank lines, you must consider the top page
margin and your page length to make sure the headers print
properly. Since the header is considered part of the top page
margin, and the default top margin is three lines, or .5 in., the
header margin plus the number of lines in the header cannot
exceed three lines or .5 in. unless you change the size of the
top margin. The calculation using the number of lines is relative to the line height setting. If you change the line height,
you must take this change into account when calculating your
margins.

SEE ALSO

Footers
Line Height
Margins
Page Numbering

Help

The following commands allow you to access WordStar's help system.

RELEASE

4 and 5

KEY SEQUENCE

To get help from the Opening menu:

F1

or, in Release 4 and Release 5, help level 3 or below:

J

To get help from within a file:

^J *or* **F1** *<control code command >*

To get help about a pull-down menu item:

[Select pull-down menu item] **^J** *or* **F1**

To get help from within a dialog box (Release 5 only):

^J *or* **F1**

USAGE

WordStar's online help system allows you to retrieve information about its commands without leaving the program. To access information about a specific command, access the

Help screen using the command listed above, and then type the command you want to learn about or, if you want information about a pull-dwon menu item, select that item and then press ^J or **F1**. A brief explanation will appear on the screen. Press the Spacebar to exit Help, or the Esc key when you are prompted to do so. For a general explanation of dot commands, press the period key (.) from the Help screen.

Setting the Help Level

These commands allow you to determine the amount and type of information and commands with which WordStar supplies you.

KEY SEQUENCE

To set the help level from the Classic Opening menu:

F1 ^J *n*

or

J ^J *n*

or, in Release 5 from the pull-down Opening menu:

Other/Change help level.../*n*

where *n* is the level number explained below.

To set the help level from within a file (Release 4 only or Release 5, help level 3):

^J ^J *n* or **F1 F1** *n* or any combination of ^j and **F1**

or (Release 5 only):

EDIT/Other/Change help level.../*n*

where *n* is the level number explained below.

USAGE

The following is a list of the various help levels and what information and command sets they provide:

4   Release 5 only: all pull-down menus, prompts, confirmations (such as *Are you sure?*) are on.

3   All Classic menus, prompts, confirmations, are on.

2   Edit menu is off; other menus are on.

1   All menus, prompts, confirmations are off.

0   All menus, prompts, confirmations, opening menu directory are off. In Release 4, the status line is also off. In Release 5, you can also copy, move, and delete hidden blocks.

Hide/Display Controls

The following commands allow you to turn the display of print control codes on and off.

RELEASE

4 and 5

KEY SEQUENCE

^OD *or* **Shift-F1**

or (Release 5 only):

EDIT/Style/Hide/display controls

To turn the display of control codes on or off, press one of the key sequences listed above. The default setting is to display codes. For instance, if a word is encoded to be printed in boldface, with controls displayed it will appear like this:

^Btext^B

with the initial code and the remaining encoded text brighter (on a monochrome screen) or in a different color. With the controls hidden, the text would still be brighter or in a different color, but the **^B** codes would become invisible. It is still possible to insert or delete codes when they are hidden, although it is somewhat tricky to determine when the cursor is on the displayed letter and when it is on the hidden code.

Hiding codes is especially useful when you are working with tabular columns of text that have either fixed position character codes to make them line up (**^P@**) or other print codes such as underlining or boldface that render the alignment difficult to determine when displayed. Soft hyphens, which appear as equal symbols when controls are displayed, also disappear when controls are hidden.

In Release 5, hiding controls also hides codes referred to as *tags*, such as comments or index entries in text or font or printer selection tags.

Dot commands are still visible when controls are hidden. To suppress their display, use Page Preview (**^OP**).

| SEE ALSO |

Hyphenation

Page Preview

Hyphenation

These commands allow you to hyphenate text.

RELEASE

4 and 5

KEY SEQUENCE

See individual sections.

USAGE

The automatic hyphenation features of Releases 4 and 5 differ substantially. If you have Release 5, see **Auto-Hyphenation**. If you have Release 4, see **Hyphen Help**. The section **Soft Hyphens** applies to both releases.

Auto-Hyphenation (Release 5 Only)

This command allows you to turn automatic hyphenation on and off.

KEY SEQUENCE

^OH

USAGE

WordStar automatically hyphenates words when they fall within a 5-character zone at the right margin, if hyphenation is possible. The size of this zone can be changed using WSCHANGE (see Appendix A). Auto-hyphenation inserts soft hyphens (see below) into the words at certain logical separating points. To turn this feature off, press **^OH**. You can still insert hyphens manually. To prevent an individual word from being hyphenated while Auto-hyphenation is on, insert a soft hyphen (**^OE**) immediately preceding it. The word will not be hyphenated.

Auto-hyphenation will not print hyphens it has inserted if, during editing, the word has moved back into the middle of a line. To insert a *hard hyphen* (one that will always print, no matter where the word falls on the line), press the hyphen (-) key.

Hyphen Help (Release 4 Only)

This command allows you to turn suggested hyphen placement on and off.

KEY SEQUENCE

^OH

USAGE

To use Hyphen Help, press **^OH**. As you are typing (or realigning a paragraph) WordStar will prompt you with a selected hyphenation when a word falls within a 5-character zone at the right margin, if hyphenation of the word is possible. The size of this zone can be changed using WSCHANGE (see Appendix A). Hyphen Help inserts soft hyphens (see below) into the words at certain logical separating points. You can use the cursor movement keys to move the hyphen to the location you feel is proper, then press -. If you don't want to hyphenate the word suggested, press **^B** to stop hyphenation but continue reformatting or **^U** to abort the entire procedure. To turn Hyphen Help off, press **^OH**. You can still insert hyphens manually. To prevent an individual word from being hyphenated while Hyphen Help is on in Release 5, insert a soft hyphen (**^OE**) immediately preceding it. The word will not be hyphenated.

WordStar will not print hyphens it has inserted if, during editing, the word has moved back into the middle of a line. To insert a *hard hyphen* (one that will always print, no matter where the word falls on the line), simply press the - key.

Soft Hyphens

This command inserts a hyphen that will print only if it occurs at the end of a line.

RELEASE

4 and 5

KEY SEQUENCE

^OE

USAGE

To insert a hyphen that will print only if it occurs at the end of a line, press **^OE**. An equal symbol (=) will appear at the cursor position if codes are set to display. This is also the type of hyphen inserted when Auto-hyphenation or Hyphen Help inserts the hyphen.

You can change the symbol for soft hyphen using the WSCHANGE program (see Appendix A).

Indent

The following command allows you to indent entire paragraphs of text.

| RELEASE |

4 and 5

| KEY SEQUENCE |

To indent text while typing:

^OG<*text* >↵

pressing **^OG** once for each tab stop to indent, and then pressing ↵ to stop.

To indent existing text, move the cursor to the beginning of the text, then:

^OG

pressing **^OG** for each tab stop to indent, then:

^B

| USAGE |

To indent a paragraph of text while typing, press **^OG**. A **V** will appear on the first standard tab stop (the tab stops displayed as exclamation points (!) on the ruler line) and the tab symbol (➤) will appear as well. When you type in text and reach the right margin, the text will wrap one tab stop in from the left margin. Each successive line of text will do the same until you end the paragraph by pressing ⏎. To indent more than one tab stop, press **^OG** repeatedly until the **V** on the ruler line appears at the desired location, and then proceed with typing. WordStar will ignore decimal tab stops in this operation. If you realign the paragraph later using **^B** or **^QU**, the indention will disappear, and the text will move flush with the left margin of the text once more.

If you want to indent an existing paragraph of text, position the cursor at the left margin (column 1) on the first line of the paragraph. Press **^OG** once for each tab stop you want the paragraph indented, as described above. When the **V** on the ruler line is at the desired location, press **^B** to realign the paragraph with the new indention. If you realign the paragraph again later, as above, the indention will disappear.

If you are using the automatic paragraph indent (the paragraph margin dot command, **.PM**), pressing **^OG** moves the indention to the first tab stop *after* (that is, to the right of) the paragraph margin (displayed as a **P** on the ruler line). It will not preserve the indention of the first line. To do this, you must use the Spacebar or Tab key to indent the paragraph.

To create a paragraph with a *hanging indent* (the first line flush with the left margin and the rest of the lines indented), position the cursor on the first line of the paragraph at the column of the indent, and then press **^OG** the appropriate number of times (followed by **^B** if you are indenting an existing paragraph). All text to the left of the cursor will remain flush with the left margin.

You can also create more permanent indentions using ruler lines and paragraph and left margin settings. See the related entries for more information.

SEE ALSO

Auto Indent

Margins

Paragraph Margins

Ruler Line

Tabs

Index

The following commands help you to create index entries and generate an index.

RELEASE

4 and 5

KEY SEQUENCE

See individual sections.

USAGE

Indexes are usually created using a two-step process. First, you select terms in your document that you consider to be important and useful as index entries. Then you generate an index of your document, which will have the same file name as your document with the extension .IDX. The index you have generated will show each selected term and all the page numbers on which it occurs. One option allows you to create an index that includes every word in your document (except for a set of commonly used words not ordinarily indexed, such as pronouns and articles). WordStar also allows you to create your own exclusion list.

Selecting Index Entries

The following commands allow you to select index entries.

KEY SEQUENCE

To select an index entry without modifying the way it appears in the text:

^PK<*text* >**^PK**

To select an index entry to be modified (or entered as a subentry):

.IX [–][+]<*main entry* >, <*subentry* >

or (in Release 5 only):

^ONI [–][+]<*main entry* >, <*subentry* >**^K** [*or* **F10** *or* ↵]

or (in Release 5 only):

EDIT/Other/Index entry.../
[–][+]<*main entry* >, <*subentry* >**^K** [*or* **F10** *or* ↵]

where – will generate a cross-reference entry (with no page numbers) and, in Release 5 only, + will cause the page number to appear in boldface.

USAGE

To mark a word or phrase to appear as a main index entry with no modifications, mark the beginning and end of the phrase with **^PK**. If you have codes set to display, the entry will appear as

^Ktext^K

and may be highlighted in reverse video, depending on your monitor.

To mark an entry that you want to modify in some way, you can either use the dot command **.IX** or, if you have Release 5, you can embed an index entry in a paragraph from the Notes menu. To use the dot command method, insert the **.IX** command on the line above the paragraph where your actual entry occurs. If the paragraph crosses over to a new page and the entry occurs on the second page, insert the **.IX** command immediately *following* the paragraph so that the page number will appear correctly when the index is generated. After typing **.IX**, you may now type a minus sign (–) if you are indicating a cross-reference and want the page number to be suppressed. Or, in Release 5, you may type a plus sign (+) to cause the page number to appear in boldface type (often used to indicate that this entry is the main one for that word or phrase). Following the – or +, if they are desired, type the word or phrase exactly as you want it to occur in the index. If you are marking a subentry, type the main entry name and then a comma followed by the subentry. When the index is generated, the subentry will appear below the main entry, indented two spaces. The subentries within each main entry will be alphabetized as well.

In Release 5, you can also insert an index entry as a note, either by pressing **^ONI** with the cursor at the point where the actual entry occurs or selecting **EDIT/Other/Index entry....** The Index dialog box appears. Type in – or + if you want to suppress or boldface the page number, and then type the entry as you want it to appear in the index. When you are finished, press **^K**, **F10**, or ↵ to exit the dialog box. If you have codes set to display, the first several letters of your entry will appear in braces within the paragraph like this:

> although the discussion focused on semiconductors **{Semiconductors,}**, the bulk of later research was

If you want to edit or view the entire index entry later, you must access the Notes menu (either by pressing **^ON** or selecting **EDIT/Other/Footnote/endnote...**) and then press **D**. If you want to find index entries of this type, you must search for them manually using the Go to a Note feature (**^ONG**) on the Notes menu to find index entries. Select **I** for index entry.

When the dialog box appears, press Tab or ^I *once* to move past the text string line and select T (tag of note only) and then **^K**, **F10**, or ↵

Index entries of any type are limited to 50 characters. You will not be warned if you mark longer entries, but any text after the 50th character will not appear in the index.

Generating an Index

These commands allow you to generate an index from a document.

KEY SEQUENCE

From the Classic Opening menu:

I *<d:\pathname\filename.ext >*

From the pull-down Opening menu, Release 5:

Other/Index... *<d:\pathname\filename.ext >*

USAGE

To generate an index, select the indexing feature from the Opening menu using one of the methods described in the key sequence section. Next, select the file you want to index, either by typing in the name or by selecting it in the directory using the cursor keys. Then press ↵. A prompt or dialog box will appear, asking whether you want to index every word. Press **Y** if you have not marked or entered individual entries into your file. WordStar will not index the words in its exclusion file, WSINDEX.XCL, such as individual letters, pronouns, and articles, nor will it index words listed in an exclusion file you create. This method of generating an index is most useful for short documents. It has some limitations: you cannot use it in conjunction with marked entries because duplicate entries will occur. For example, if on page 6 you have inserted the entry

.IX Versailles (restoration of)

above a paragraph containing the word *Versailles*, two entries will be generated for that word, even though it is mentioned only once:

Versailles, 6
Versailles (restoration of), 6

This method can therefore only successfully index individual words (no phrases), and it won't allow you to create cross-references, subentries, or boldface page numbers (Release 5).

If you have marked entries throughout your document, answer **N** to the prompt *Index every word*.

After the *Index every word* prompt, WordStar will allow you to specify the page numbers you want indexed. If you want to index the entire document, press **Esc** at this point in Release 4 or **^K** or **F10** in Release 5 to begin generating the index. If you want to specify pages to be indexed in Release 4, you can specify a starting and an ending page. In Release 5, you can specify a range of pages using a hyphen (**-**) to separate the numbers (such as **3-8**) or commas (**,**) to separate individually specified pages (such as **5,7,18**). You can also combine these methods (**5-6,8,10**). Release 5 also lets you specify whether all pages (**a**), even pages only (**e**), or odd pages only (**o**) should be indexed. Use **Tab** and **Shift-Tab** to move among the various options in the Index dialog box and press **^K** or **F10** when done. You can abandon the entire indexing process by pressing **^U**.

To create your own exclusion file, open a nondocument file and give it the same name as the file you want to index, but with the file name extension **.XCL**. Type in the words and phrases you want excluded from your index in ascending alphabetical order, pressing ↵ after each entry. Save the file in the usual manner, and then generate your index.

SEE ALSO

Copy

Delete

Notes

Rename

Insert Mode

This command turns the Insert mode on and off.

RELEASE

4 and 5

KEY SEQUENCE

^V *or* **Ins**

USAGE

WordStar's *Insert mode* normally allows you to insert text at
the cursor position, pushing everything to the right of the cursor
without erasing it. When you are editing in Insert mode,
the word "Insert" will appear on the status line. If you want
to type over everything at and to the right of the cursor, type
^V or **Ins** to turn Insert mode off. While Insert mode is off,
pressing **^I** or the **Tab** key will move the cursor over only to
the next tab stop; it will not push text to the right. Even if Insert
is off, moving a block to where text is already in place will

not erase the text at the block move's destination, unless you are using the Column Block feature and Column Replace is turned on, in which case the block will be replaced whether Insert is on or off.

| SEE ALSO |

Block Operations

Insert a File

See **Block Operations: Read Block.**

Installation

See **Appendix A.**

Italics

These commands allow you to print in italics if your printer can do so.

RELEASE

5 only

KEY SEQUENCE

^PY<*text* >**^PY**

or

EDIT/Style/Italics/<*text* >EDIT/Style/Italics

USAGE

This feature is not supported by all printers (for example, daisy-wheel). Check your printer documentation to see if it is capable of printing italics. To italicize text, press **^PY** or select **EDIT/Style/Italics** where you want the italics to begin and the same command once more where you want them to end. If you have control codes hidden, the text that you have italicized will appear brighter or in a different color. If you have control codes displayed, **^Y** markers will also appear where you inserted the codes. To remove italics, simply delete the codes. Italics can be combined with other print controls such as underlining or boldface, although your printer may not be capable of printing all combinations.

SEE ALSO

Hide/Display Controls

Italics/Color

This command allows you to print text in italics or in two colors in Release 4. For the corresponding commands in Release 5, see **Color Printing** and **Italics**.

RELEASE

4 only

KEY SEQUENCE

^PY<*text* >**^PY**

USAGE

This feature prints either in italics or in a second color, depending on the type and capability of your printer; it is not supported by all printers (for example, daisy-wheel). Check your printer documentation to see if your printer is capable of printing italics or with a two-color ribbon. To italicize text or print it in a second color, press **^PY** where you want the italics or second color to begin and the same command once more where you want it to end. If you have control codes hidden, the text that you have selected will appear brighter or in a different color. If you have control codes displayed, **^Y** markers will also appear where you inserted the codes. To remove italics or the second color, simply delete the codes. Italics/Color can be combined with other print controls such as underlining or boldface, although your printer may not be capable of printing all combinations.

SEE ALSO

Color Printing

Italics

Hide/Display Controls

Landscape and Portrait Modes

These commands allow you to switch between Landscape mode (where the text is rotated 90 degrees and printed sideways) and Portrait Mode (the standard setting).

RELEASE

5 only

KEY SEQUENCE

To print in Landscape mode:

.PR OR=L

To return to Portrait mode:

.PR OR=P

USAGE

Landscape mode is chiefly available on laser printers; check your printer documentation to see if your printer supports this page orientation. To print in Landscape mode, insert the dot command **.PR OR=L** at the top of the page. Remember to adjust the page length and right margin settings accordingly. If you are using 8 1/2 × 11-inch paper, set the page length to 8.5 inches and the right margin to 9.6 inches by inserting the lines

.PL 8.5"
.RM 9.6"

If you change back to Portrait mode in the same document, make sure you do so on a new page; printers cannot use both modes on the same page. Also, don't forget to reset the page length and right margins to their usual settings.

Line Feed

This command inserts a line feed code into your file.

RELEASE

4 and 5

KEY SEQUENCE

^PJ

USAGE

To insert a line feed, press **^PJ** at the location at which you want the printer to move down a line. A **J** will appear in the flag column, and the rest of the text on that line will move down to the next line on the screen. When printed, the document will move down a line at the **^PJ** location and continue printing the rest of the line at that cursor position without starting the new line at the left margin.

SEE ALSO

Form Feed

Line Height

This command allows you to adjust the space between printed lines of text.

RELEASE

4 and 5

KEY SEQUENCE

.LH *n*

where *n* is the height of the line in 48ths of an inch.

USAGE

To change the space between printed lines of text (line height), insert the **.LH** command, followed by the line height in 48ths of an inch. The default, single-spaced line height setting in WordStar prints 6 lines to the inch; the corresponding line height command would be **.LH 8**. To print double-spaced text (three lines per inch), insert the command **.LH 16**. The line height can be any number from 2 to 255. Although the line height changes when printed, text will still appear single-spaced on-screen, although page breaks will be adjusted to appear in the appropriate places. With Release 5 and a graphics monitor, you can preview the appearance of the page using Page Preview (**^OP**).

You can also use the Line Spacing command to change the line height of your document. See that entry for more details.

SEE ALSO

Line Spacing

Line Numbering

The following command adds line numbering to your printed document.

RELEASE

5 only

KEY SEQUENCE

.**L#** [d][p]<*spacing* >,<*column* >

USAGE

To number lines of text (for legal documents, for instance) use the **.L#** command. Insert the command on the line above the first line to be numbered. In the printed document, single or double vertical lines will appear between the line numbers and the left margin, and a single vertical line will appear to the right of the right margin. The default numbering system starts renumbering at the top of each page. If you want consecutive numbering throughout the document, press **d** after typing **.L#**. Next, type the spacing you want for line numbering; if you want numbering to occur every line, type **1**; if you want it to occur every two lines, type **2**, and so forth. If you don't specify spacing or type **0**, line numbering will be turned off. Please note that if you select numbering every two lines or more, the numbers will not have a one-to-one correspondence to the lines. That is, if you type **.L#2**, the first line will be numbered 1, the second will have no number, the third will be numbered 2, and so on. Next, type a comma followed by the number of spaces to the left of the margin to designate the column at which the line numbers will be printed. If you specify no column, the number will print three spaces to the left of the margin.

If you want to return to renumbering at the top of every page, insert **.L# p** at the top of that page followed by the spacing and line numbering column. If you insert a line numbering column in the middle of a page, the new command will not take effect until the following page. To turn line numbering off, insert the command **.L# 0** at the top of the page you want printed with no line numbering.

You can reset the default page column and change the default numbering from renumbering at the top of each page to numbering consecutively throughout the document with WSCHANGE. See Appendix A for details.

SEE ALSO

Paragraph Numbering

Appendix A

Line Spacing

The following commands allow you to change the line spacing in your document.

RELEASE

4 and 5

KEY SEQUENCE

To change line spacing in Release 4:

^OS *n*

or

.LS *n*

where *n* is a number between 1 and 9.

To change line spacing in Release 5:

.LS *n*

or

^OS *n* ↵ [*or* **^K** *or* **F10**]

or

EDIT/Layout/Single/double spacing.../*n* ↵ [*or* **^K** *or* **F10**]

where *n* is the number of spaces (1–9) between lines plus 1.

USAGE

To change line spacing (on-screen as well as on the printed page) in Release 4, you can either use a control command (**^OS**) or a dot command (**.LS**). In Release 5, you can also access the feature from the EDIT/Layout pull-down menu. In all cases, after entering the command, type the number that corresponds with the amount of spacing you want in your file. For instance, if you want double spacing, type **2**. If you want triple spacing, type **3** and so on, up to 9. If you are using Release 5, pressing **^OS** or selecting **Single/double spacing...**

from the EDIT/Layout menu will bring up the MARGINS & TABS dialog box with the cursor in the Line spacing section. Using **Tab** and **Shift-Tab** to move around within the dialog box, you may make other changes to your margins and tabs at this time by not pressing ↵, **^K**, or **F10** immediately after entering the spacing number.

If you are changing the line spacing of existing text, you must reformat the affected paragraphs using **^B** or **^QU**.

TIP

If you want to set your line spacing in increments smaller than a line, use the line height command, **.LH**; see the entry above. The line height command does not display the line spacing on-screen, but it can be set in 48ths of an inch and takes up less memory because with the line spacing command every extra line is literally added to the file as a blank line, whereas with the line height command the spacing is performed only at print time. This also means that using both line height and line spacing commands at the same time should be avoided, since they do not cancel each other out, but rather multiply each others' effects.

SEE ALSO

Line Height

Loading WordStar

See **Starting WordStar.**

Lowercase

See **Case Conversion.**

Macros

See **Shorthand.**

MailList

The following commands allow you to access the MailList database/mailing list program.

RELEASE

5 only

KEY SEQUENCE

From the Classic Opening menu:

AM

From the pull-down Opening menu:

Additional/MailList...

From the DOS prompt:

WSLIST

USAGE

To access the MailList program, type one of the key sequences listed above from the Opening menu or **WSLIST** from the DOS prompt. This program can operate from within Word-Star or by itself as a simple inventory and mailing list database program with predesigned forms for individual records. A detailed description of this program is outside the scope of this book, however. Refer to the section on MailList in your WordStar documentation.

MailMerge

See **Merge Print.**

Margin Release

This command allows you to type beyond the right margin temporarily.

RELEASE

4 and 5

---

^OX

or (in Release 5 only):

EDIT/Layout/Margin release

| USAGE |

To release the right margin temporarily (preventing the text from wrapping to the next line), press **^OX** or select **EDIT/Layout/Margin release**. The message *Mar-Rel* will appear on the status line to let you know the margin release feature is in effect. The command stays in effect as long as you extend your line past the right margin or until you move your cursor to another line or press ↵. Pressing **^B** or **^QU** will realign text within the margins.

Margins

The following commands allow you to set the top, bottom, left, and right margins of your page. For information on changing your footer, header, and paragraph margins and page offset and page length settings, see the appropriate sections.

| RELEASE |

4 and 5

KEY SEQUENCE ═══════════════

See individual sections.

USAGE ═══════════════

There are several ways to set the page margins in WordStar. These features behave differently in Releases 4 and 5. In Release 4, you can insert some margins with control commands temporarily. In Release 5, all margin settings require inserting dot commands in the file. Consult the individual sections for more information on how this works.

Setting the Top Margin

The following commands allow you to change the top margin of your document.

KEY SEQUENCE ═══════════════

To set the top margin using lines as a unit of measurement:

.MT *n*

where *n* is the number of lines in the top margin.

To set the top margin using inches as a unit of measurement (in Release 5 only):

.MT *n.nn"*

or

^OL Tab Tab Tab *n.nn* **^K** [*or* **F10**]

or

EDIT/Layout/Margins and tabs.../
Tab Tab Tab *n.nn* **^K** [*or* **F10**]

where *n.nn* is the number of inches in the top margin.

To change the top margin of your document using lines (the only method available in Release 4), insert the dot command **.MT** with the number of lines you want in your top margin. The default top margin is 3 lines, if you are using the standard line height. (A line height command preceding a top margin command using lines as units will change the value of the top margin command. The standard line height is 8/48 in. (.LH8). If you change this setting, lines will no longer be 8/48 in. high, and you must adjust your calculations based on the new line height.)

For example, to increase the top margin to 2 in., insert

.MT 12

at the top of the page. Since there are 6 lines to an inch with the default line height, 12 lines equals 2 in. This command will decrease the number of lines of text you can fit on a page by 9 lines, since we have increased the margin by 9 lines (1.50 in.).

To change the top margin of your document using inches, an option in Release 5 only, insert the dot command **.MT** with the margin you want expressed in number of inches and hundredths of inches followed by the inch symbol ("), or access the MARGINS & TABS dialog box either by pressing **^OL** or selecting **Margins and tabs...** from the EDIT/Layout pull-down menu, and use the Tab key to move the cursor down to the top margin setting. The default top margin is .50 in. Enter the new setting here and then press **^K** or **F10**; it is not necessary to type the " symbol when entering the new margin from the MARGINS & TABS dialog box.

The new setting will appear as a dot command in your document.

For example, to increase the top margin to 2 in., insert

.MT 2"

at the top of the page, or select the top margin setting in the MARGINS & TABS dialog box, press **2** and then **^K** or **F10**.

Setting the Bottom Margin

The following commands allow you to change the bottom margin of your document.

KEY SEQUENCE

To set the bottom margin using lines as a unit of measure:

  .MB *n*

where *n* is the number of lines in the bottom margin.

To set the bottom margin using inches as a unit of measurement (in Release 5 only):

  .MB *n.nn"*

or

  ^OL [Select Margins, Bottom] *n.nn* **^K** [*or* **F10**]

or

  EDIT/Layout/Margins and tabs.../
  [Select Margins, Bottom] *n.nn* **^K** [*or* **F10**]

where *n.nn* is the number of inches in the bottom margin.

USAGE

To change the bottom margin of your document using lines (the only method available in Release 4), insert the dot command **.MB** with the number of lines you want in your bottom margin. The default bottom margin is 8 lines, if you are using the standard line height. (A line height preceding a bottom margin command using lines as units will change the value of the bottom margin command. The standard line height is 8/48 in. (.LH8). If you change this setting, lines will no longer be 8/48 in. high, and you must adjust your calculations based on the new line height.)

For example, to increase the bottom margin to 3 in., insert the line

.MB 18

at the top of the page. Since there are 6 lines to an inch with the default line height, 18 lines equals 3 in. This command will decrease the number of lines of text you can fit on a page by 10 lines, since we have increased the margin by 10 lines (1.66 in.).

To change the bottom margin of your document using inches (an option in Release 5 only), insert the dot command **.MB** with the margin you want expressed in number of inches and hundredths of inches followed by the inch symbol ("), or access the MARGINS & TABS dialog box either by pressing **^OL** or selecting **Margins and tabs...** from the EDIT/Layout pull-down menu and use the Tab key to move the cursor down to the bottom margin setting. The default bottom margin is 1.33 in.

Enter the new setting here and then press **^K** or **F10**; it is not necessary to type the " symbol when entering the new margin from the MARGINS & TABS dialog box.

The new setting will appear as a dot command in your document.

For example, to increase the bottom margin to 3 in., insert the line

.MB 3"

at the top of the page, or select the bottom margin setting in the MARGINS & TABS dialog box, press **3** and then **^K** or **F10**.

Setting the Left Margin

The following commands allow you to change the left margin of your document. (You can also change it using an embedded ruler line. See **Ruler Line** for more information on this method.)

KEY SEQUENCE

To set the left margin using columns as a unit of measurement:

.LM *n*

or (in Release 4 only):

^OL *n*

where *n* is the column number (1–255) of the left margin.

To set the left margin at the current cursor position (Release 4 only):

^OL Esc

To set the left margin using inches as a unit of measurement (in Release 5 only):

.LM *n.nn"*

or

^OL *n.nn* **^K** [*or* **F10**]

or

EDIT/Layout/Margins and tabs.../
n.nn **^K** [*or* **F10**]

where *n.nn* is the distance in inches from column 1.

USAGE

To set the left margin within a document using columns as a unit of measurement (the only option in Release 4), insert the dot command **.LM** followed by the column number of the left margin. The default left margin is column 1. (The actual default page margin of 1 in. can be adjusted using the Page Offset commands; see that section for more information). The **L** on the ruler line will move to that column whenever your cursor moves below the line containing the **.LM** command, and any text following the command will begin at the new left margin—with the exception of dot commands, which always begin on column 1. The ➤ symbol will appear to indicate the new indent. If you save the document and edit it later, this left margin setting will be preserved until you delete it. If you change the margin of existing text, you must realign the text to make it conform to the new margin using **^B** or **^QL**.

If you have Release 4 and want to change the left margin temporarily, use **^OL** followed by the column number of the new left margin. This new left margin remains in effect for the current document and editing session only, or until you change it again. The chief difference from the dot command is that if you realign the paragraph later, it will return to the default left margin. You can also set a new left margin temporarily at the cursor position by pressing **^OL Esc**.

To set the left margin using inches as a unit of measurement (an option available only in Release 5), either insert the dot command **.LM** followed by the distance in inches and the inch symbol ("), or access the MARGINS & TABS dialog box by pressing **^OL** or selecting **Margins and tabs...** from the EDIT/Layout pull-down menu, and then type in the new margin number expressed in inches and press **^K** or **F10** (you needn't type the " symbol using this method).

Setting the Right Margin

The following commands allow you to change the right margin of your document. (You can also change it using an embedded ruler line. See **Ruler Line** for more information on this method.)

KEY SEQUENCE ▭ ══════════

To set the right margin using columns as a unit of measurement:

   .RM *n*

or (in Release 4 only):

   ^OR *n*

where *n* is the column number (1–255) of the right margin.

To set the right margin at the current cursor position (Release 4 only):

   ^OR Esc

To set the right margin using inches as a unit of measurement:

   .RM *n.nn"*

or

   ^OR *n.nn* **^K** [*or* **F10**]

or

   EDIT/Layout/Margins and tabs.../
   Tab *n.nn* **^K** [*or* **F10**]

where *n.nn* is the distance in inches from column 1.

USAGE ▭ ══════════

To set the right margin within a document using columns as a unit of measurement (the only option in Release 4), insert the dot command **.RM** followed by the column number of the right margin. The default right margin is column 65. The **R** on the ruler line will move to that column whenever your cursor moves below the line containing the **.RM** command, and any text following the command will wrap according to the new right margin. If you save the document and edit it later, this right margin setting will be preserved until you delete it.

If you change the margin of existing text, you must realign the text to make it conform to the new margin using **^B** or **^QU**.

To set the right margin using inches as a unit of measurement (an option available only in Release 5), either insert the dot command **.RM** followed by the distance in inches and the inch symbol (**"**), or access the MARGINS & TABS dialog box by pressing **^OR** or selecting **Margins and tabs...** from the EDIT/Layout pull-down menu, and then type in the new margin number expressed in inches and press **^K** or **F10** (you needn't type the **"** symbol using this method). If you use the MARGINS & TABS dialog box, the **.RM** dot command as well as the bottom, footer, and header margin commands (**.MB**, **.FM**, **.HM**, respectively) will appear in your document, using the current settings.

SEE ALSO

Footers

Headers

Page Length

Page Offset

Paragraph Margins

Ruler Line

Markers

This command allows you to insert nonprinting place markers in your document.

RELEASE

4 and 5

KEY SEQUENCE

To insert a place marker in the text:

^K *n*

where *n* is a number 0–9.

To go to a place marker:

^Q *n*

where *n* is the number of a place marker previously set in that document.

USAGE

To insert a place marker, position your cursor at the location you want to keep track of and press **^K** followed by a number (0–9). The number will appear on your screen in reverse video or in a different color. You can have up to ten markers at any time. If you use a number a second time, the first marker will disappear. You can turn the display of these markers on and off by pressing **^KH** or **Shift-F6**, the display/hide block command. These place markers are for a single editing session only; if you exit a file, they disappear.

To find a marker in a file, press **^Q** followed by the number of the marker you want to find. The cursor will move to that position in the file very quickly, even if you have hidden the marker with the display/hide block command.

Math

See **Block Operations: Block Math** *and* **Calculator.**

Merge Print

The following commands allow you to merge data into a file at print time.

RELEASE

4 and 5

KEY SEQUENCE

To merge print a file from the Opening menu in Release 4:

M<*d:\pathname\filename.ext* >↵
           Number of copies? [**Esc** to accept default
                         values]
  Pause between pages (Y/N)?
    Use form feeds (Y/N)?
       Starting page?
        Ending page?
    Nondocument (Y/N)?
     Name of printer?

To merge print a file from the Classic Opening menu in Release 5:

> **M**<*d:\pathname\filename.ext* >↵ [select print options]
> **^K** [*or* **F10**]

or from the pull-down Opening menu:

> File/Merge print a file.../
> <*d:\pathname\filename.ext* >↵ [select print options]
> **^K** [*or* **F10**]

To merge print a file during editing in Release 4:

> **^KP**
>   Merge print (Y/N)? **Y**
>   Document to merge print? <*d:\pathname\filename.ext* >
>   Number of copies? [**Esc** to accept default
>   values]
> Pause between pages (Y/N)?
>   Use form feeds (Y/N)?
>   Starting page?
>   Ending page?
>   Nondocument (Y/N)?
>   Name of printer?

To merge print a file from within a file in Release 5:

> **^KPM**<*d:\pathname\filename.ext* >↵ [select print
> options] **^K** [*or* **F10**]

or

> EDIT/File/Merge print a file.../
> <*d:\pathname\filename.ext* >↵ [select print options]
> **^K** [*or* **F10**]

USAGE

Merge printing combines (merges) data from one file (the *data file*) into a template file containing boilerplate text, variables, and merge printing codes (the *master file*) to generate a new document or several documents at print time. To initiate a merge print operation, type the appropriate key sequence from the list above, selecting your master file as the file to print. Next, select any print options by answering the questions in Release 4 or using the Tab key to make changes in the MERGE PRINT dialog box in Release 5. These options behave like those in the standard printing mode. See **Print** for more information. If you try to print using the standard print command, WordStar will print your variable names rather than the data with which you want to replace them.

A brief explanation of the merge printing commands is included in the sections below. The merge printing commands in WordStar are numerous and powerful enough to allow you to create elaborate routines; they can also be combined with the MailList feature. A thorough description of the many possible routines is outside the scope of this book. See your WordStar documentation for a more complete explanation and set of examples.

Data Files

The following commands allow you to specify data files from within master files. See **Nondocument Mode** for more details on how to create a data file.

KEY SEQUENCE

To specify a data file from within a master file:

.DF *<d:\pathname\filename:ext >* **[c]**, <data separator>

To specify a data file from a Lotus 1-2-3, Symphony, or Quattro spreadsheet (in Release 5 only):

.DF *<d:\pathname\filename:ext >* **[c]**,
<cell range >,<window >

USAGE

To perform a merge print operation, you must specify a data file from which data will replace your declared variables (unless you are using only predefined variables, variables with data inserted in the master file (**.SV**), or variables with data typed in from the keyboard at print time (**.AV**)).

The data file can be

- a WordStar nondocument file
- a MailList file
- a dBASE III or dBASE III PLUS file
- a Lotus 1-2-3 (not Version 3) file
- a Symphony spreadsheet file
- a Quattro spreadsheet file
- a comma-delimited ASCII text file

To create a data file within WordStar, open a nondocument file (see **Nondocument Mode**) and insert a list of data separated by commas, hard carriage returns (↵), or another character you have designated as a data separator, for each copy of the master document you wish to produce. The data must be in the same order as it is in the read variable command in your master file, and any blank field must be taken up by an extra data separator (usually a comma). For instance, if you have the variable list

.RV firstname,lastname,company,address,city,state,zip

in your master file, and you are sending one copy of the document to Jane Michaels, who is not affiliated with any company, you would enter

Jane,Michaels,,312 State Street,Pasadena,CA,91001

Note the additional comma preceding the address, indicating that there is no company for this record. There should be no space between the commas. If you want to incorporate data containing commas, enclose the data in quotation marks (" ").

Once you have created the data file, you must specify it within the master file immediately preceding the read variable command. If the data file is on another disk, you can have WordStar prompt you to change disks by typing **c** after the file name.

You can choose a different character to act as the data separator; just type a comma after you specify the file name in the data file command (**.DF**), and then type the character you want to use instead.

You can also use data files created by other programs. WordStar recognizes the various file formats you can use for data files; you need not specify the format. If you are using a spreadsheet file, WordStar assumes you are using the first or main window. You can also specify a cell range. If you want to select a range from a starting cell to the end of a file, use the asterisk in your range setting. For instance, if you want to use a 1-2-3 file starting from B14 and going to the end of the file, type **,B14..*** after the file name (and change disks switch if there is one). If you are using a dBASE file, WordStar uses dBASE field names for its variable names.

Variables

The following commands allow you to create variables within a master document that will print the corresponding text from your data files at print time.

KEY SEQUENCE

To insert a variable into a master document:

&_<variable>_**&**

where _variable_ is a string of letters or numbers up to 39 characters in length with no commas or slashes (/).

To insert the current page number into a master document:

&#&

To insert the current line number into a master document:

&_&

To insert the current system date into a master document:

&@&

To insert the current system time into a master document:

&!&

To insert a cell value from a spreadsheet into a master document (in Release 5 only):

&<cell name >**&**

To read (declare) a list of variables contained in a data file:

.RV <variable1,variable2,variable3,...etc.>

To read a partial list of variables contained in a data file (in Release 5 only):

.RV* <variable1,variable2,variable3,...etc.>

USAGE

To insert a merge print variable into your master document, position your cursor at the point at which you want the variable information to occur in your printed document and type the appropriate variable name surrounded by ampersands (&). You can change the variable symbol to something other than an ampersand with WSCHANGE (see Appendix A). If your variable occurs in the middle of a paragraph, WordStar will automatically realign the paragraph to accommodate the varying lengths of the data that replace your variable unless otherwise specified (see **Align Paragraphs** for more details). You can control the position of merge print variables more precisely using variable formatting in dot commands. See the appropriate section below for details.

Standard variables that you define must appear in the master file in a list following the read-variable dot command

(**.RV**) (see **Data Files** below). Predefined variables for the current page, line, date, and time, math variables (**.MA**), and variables set with **.SV** or **.AV** need not be specified in the read variable command.

To read a list of data, you must insert into the master file the read-variable dot command (**.RV**) followed by a list of all the variables in the data file, separated by commas. The **.RV** command must follow the data file dot command (**.DF)** to work properly. All the variables listed must appear in the same order they appear in the data file. In Release 5, you can use a partial list in the read variable dot command if you insert an asterisk between the dot command and the variable list. The partial list must include all the variables up to and including the last one you want to use, even if you will not use all the variables in that range. In other words, if you want to use only *variable2*, *variable3*, and *variable5* in your merge operation, you must specify them as follows in the read variable command:

.RV* <*variable1*,*variable2*,*variable3*,*variable4*,*variable5*>

Using a partial list in a read variable command will function properly only if a comma is used as the data separator; you cannot use it with data files where data is separated by carriage returns.

If you are using a spreadsheet file as a data file, the variable names are the column letters or row numbers preceded by a dollar sign ($). For instance, to print the entries for two variables as the values in columns C and H of a Lotus 1-2-3 spreadsheet, you would type

.RV* **$C,$H**

If a value will be the same for each merged record, you can assign a specific cell, such as **$C47**. In all cases, make sure that the dollar sign also appears where the variable occurs in the master file, such as **&$C&**. With a spreadsheet file, you need not specify all columns or rows up to and including the last one you used, as you must do with other types of data files.

Ask for Variable

The following command allows you to be prompted to type in information during the merge print operation.

KEY SEQUENCE

To ask for the value of a variable at print time:

.AV *<variable >*

To ask for the value of a variable using a specific text prompt at print time:

.AV "*<text >*",*<variable >*

USAGE

To type in the value of an individual variable at print time, insert the command **.AV** in your master file. The text that you type in will appear wherever you have designated it by the variable name in the document enclosed in ampersands (&variable&). If you want the prompt to be simply the variable name followed by a question mark, type **.AV** followed by the variable name. If you want to designate a more specific text prompt, type **.AV** followed by the prompt enclosed in quotes, and then followed by a comma and the variable name. If you want to use the quote symbol (") in your prompt, enclose the entire prompt in single apostrophes (') instead of quote marks. The prompt will not appear immediately unless you are using background printing. Otherwise, the message

Print Wait

is displayed on the screen, and you must access the Printing menu by pressing **M** or **P** (or selecting **File/Merge print a file...**) on the Opening menu or by pressing **^KPM** (or selecting **EDIT/File/Merge print a file...** from the Edit screen). You will then see the prompt.

The length of the response to the prompt is limited to the total width of screen including the prompt, so if you anticipate inserting a lengthy value, make sure you use a short prompt. If you have a screen that is wider than the standard 80 characters, the prompt plus the value with which you respond can be correspondingly longer, but the value can be no longer than 80 characters no matter how wide your screen display is.

If you are using this command with a data file, you will be prompted to type in a value for each document you are generating from the data file.

Set Variable

The following command allows you to set the value of one or more variables within a master file.

KEY SEQUENCE

To set a variable occurring in a master file:

   .SV *<variable >,<text >*

To set a variable occurring in a master file with spaces in front of the variable:

   .SV *<variable >="<desired spaces ><text >"*

or

   .SV *<variable >='<desired spaces ><text >'*

USAGE

If you have a document that you frequently print and it is sometimes necessary to change one or two words or phrases in it, this command is convenient. To set a variable, type **.SV** followed by the variable name, a comma, and then the text to replace the variable. Since WordStar will ignore the spaces preceding the text in this format, type the variable name followed by an equal sign and then the text preceded by leading spaces enclosed in quotes or apostrophes, as shown above.

The set variable command is also used in the print formatting of variables; see **Variable Formatting** below for more details.

Math Variable

The following command allows you to perform mathematical calculations on variables and insert the results as text in your file during a merge print operation.

KEY SEQUENCE

.MA *<variable >=<equation >*

or

.MA *<variable >,<equation >*

where *equation* is a mathematical equation using the conventions of the Calculator (Math) function.

USAGE

To use the math variable command, insert **.MA** in your master file, followed by the name of the variable to which you want to assign the result of the calculation. The result will appear in your text wherever you have inserted that variable name in your text enclosed by ampersands (&). You can use other variables in your equation as long as you enclose them in ampersands. You can also use variables generated from other math variable equations within your master file. The most common application of this feature is to record a grand total derived from subtotals. For instance, the following set of commands renders a subtotal and a grand total that includes tax and freight when the master invoice file is printed:

.DF INVOICE
.RV item1,item2,item3,freight
.MA subtotal = &item1& + &item2& + &item3&
.MA tax = &subtotal& * .05
.MA total = &subtotal& + &tax& + &freight&

Conditional Merge Commands

The following commands allow you to insert data into merge printing files if certain specific logical conditions are met.

KEY SEQUENCE

To specify an IF condition in a merge print operation:

.IF *<condition >*

To terminate an IF condition operation in a merge print operation:

.EI

To specify an ELSE condition in a merge print operation:

.EL

To skip to the end of a file in a conditional operation:

.GO b [*or* **.GO bottom**]

To skip to the beginning of a file in a conditional operation:

.GO t [*or* **.GO top**]

USAGE

To perform a conditional merge print operation, you must specify one or more logical conditions or criteria to be met in order for an operation to be performed. The conditions are limited to mathematical and text comparisons of variables in your merge print operation. The logical operators used to express these conditions of comparison are listed in the table below.

OPERATOR	DEFINITION
=	is the same as
<	precedes alphabetically
	follows alphabetically
<=	precedes or is the same as alphabetically
=	follows or is the same as alphabetically
<>	is not the same as
#=	equals numerically
#<	is less than numerically
#>	is greater than numerically
#<=	is less than or equal to numerically
#>=	is greater than or equal to numerically
#<>	is not equal to numerically

To perform an operation *if* a specific condition is met, specify the condition in the **.IF** command, using the following form:

.IF *<value > <operator> <value >*
<dot command or text string >
.EI

where **.EI** signals the end of the **.IF** operation. For example, to express the condition "If the customer balance variable &custbal& is greater than $500, print the message: 'Carrying a higher balance makes you eligible for our special lower interest rates!'" you would type

.IF &custbal& #> 500
Carrying a higher balance makes you eligible for our
special lower interest rates!
.EI

You can also specify an alternative operation. In the example above, to add an alternative operation when the **.IF**
condition is not met: "If the customer balance variable
&custbal& is less than or equal to $500, print the message:
'Take advantage of our special lower interest rates on higher
balances! Call our toll-free information number for more
details.'" you would type

.IF &custbal& #> 500
Carrying a higher balance makes you eligible for our
special lower interest rates!
.EL
Take advantage of our special lower interest rates on
higher balances! Call our toll-free information number
for more details.
.EI

To cause the merge operation to skip to the beginning or
end of a file during a conditional merge command, use **.GO
bottom** or **.GO top**. (You can abbreviate these commands as
.GO b and **.GO t**.)

Variable Formatting

The following commands allow you to control the printed
format of merge print variables.

KEY SEQUENCE

To close up blank lines in a list of variables when no value is
given for the designated variable in a master file:

&<*variable* >/**o&**

To define a variable format in a master file:

.SV *x=<variable format >*

where *x* is any letter or number except the letter "o" or "O" (WordStar does not distinguish between upper- and lower-case here).

To assign a variable format to a variable in a master file:

&*<variable >/x***&**

where *x* is a variable format previously defined using the **.SV** command.

USAGE

To close up blank lines in a list of variables (for example, to close up the space when an address is only three lines and you have allowed space for four), type **/o** (the letter "o", not zero) after the variable name in your master file. As noted in the entry on **Data Files**, this variable must be designated as empty by the insertion of an extra comma in the data file where a value would otherwise be typed, or by pressing ↵ alone when prompted to supply a value when using the ask variable (**.AV**) command.

To define other specific formats for variables in a merge print operation, you must first define the variable format using the set variable command (**.SV**) and assigning a number or a letter other than "o" or "O" to the variable format. Then assign that variable format to the specific variable by typing a slash (/) followed by the variable format's number or letter.

The following is a list of variable format codes to be used in defining variable formats with **.SV**:

CODE   USAGE

Text format codes:

L	Print left-justified
R	Print right-justified
C	Print centered

Numeric format codes:

9	Print numeral, if any, or zero here
Z	Print numeral, if any, or space here
*	Print numeral, if any, or asterisk (to left of decimal) or zero (to right of decimal)
$	Print dollar sign, numeral, space (if any) to left of dollar sign
−	Print minus to left of first numeral, then numeral, if any, or space (unless leading zero)
.	Print decimal point here
,	Print comma here
( )	Enclose negative value in parentheses, otherwise, print spaces

For example, to define text variable format 6 as twenty characters to be printed starting from the right margin, first type

.SV 6=RRRRRRRRRRRRRRRRRRRR

Then position the variable in your master file and assign it variable format 6:

&variable/6&

If a variable's value is longer than the number of characters specified for that variable, the remainder of the characters will not be printed. If you use a character other than a text variable format code in the format definition, that character will print instead of the corresponding character in the variable. For instance, if you define the variable format as

.SV 7=LLLLLL***

and the value for your variable is "MARKETING", it will print left-justified as

MARKET***

Numeric format codes work in much the same way as text format codes. For example, to define the variable format *d* to print a number seven digits long with a decimal point after five digits and leading zeros if the number is less than seven digits in size, type

   .SV d=99999.99

If the variable is

   2345.8

it will print as

   02345.80

SEE ALSO

   Calculator
   Command Files
   MailList

Microjustification

See **Column Alignment**.

Move

See **Block Operations**.

New Page

See **Page Breaks**.

Newspaper Columns

See **Columns**.

Nondocument Mode

These commands allow you to open files in *nondocument mode,* a file format that excludes page and print formatting codes.

RELEASE

4 and 5

KEY SEQUENCE

To open any file in nondocument mode from the Opening menu in Release 4, or to open and name a file or open an existing file in nondocument mode from the Classic Opening menu in Release 5:

N<*d:\pathname\filename.ext* >

To open a file in nondocument mode from the Opening menu in Release 5 using pull-down menus:

File/Open a nondocument file.../
<*d:\pathname\filename.ext* >

To open a file in nondocument mode from the DOS prompt in Release 4:

D>WS <*d:\pathname\filename.ext* > **N**

To open a file in nondocument mode from the DOS prompt in Release 5:

D>WS <*d:\pathname\filename.ext* > /**N**

USAGE

WordStar has two file formats, *document mode* and *nondocument mode*. Document mode is the standard file format; it inserts page and print formatting and enhancements. Most printed documents are best produced in document mode. Nondocument mode is primarily used for command files, data files, and plain text files used in programming language code or read by another word processing program.

To open an existing nondocument file from the Classic Opening menu, press **N** and type in the name of the file (including drive and directory if different from the current one). You can also select a file by pressing ^X or ↓ to move from the prompt line to the directory and then using the cursor keys to select the appropriate file. When the cursor is on the correct file, press ↵.

To open a new nondocument file from the Classic Opening menu, press **N** as above and type in the new file name. You will see the following prompt (unless you are using help level 0 or 1, in which case WordStar creates the file automatically if it doesn't already exist):

Can't find that file. Create a new one (Y/N)?

Answer **Y** and a new file will be opened.

SEE ALSO

Document Mode

Merge Print

Save

Speed Write

Notes

The following commands allow you to insert various types of notes into your document.

RELEASE

5 only

KEY SEQUENCE

To insert an annotation into your document:

^ONA<annotation mark >↵
[or **^K** or **F10**]
<text >**^KD**[or **F10**]

or

>   EDIT/Other/Footnote/endnote.../**A**
>   *<text>*^**KD**

To insert a nonprinting comment into your document:

>   ^**ONC***<text>*^**KD**

or

>   EDIT/Other/Footnote/endnote.../**C**
>   *<text>*^**KD**

To insert an endnote into your document:

>   ^**ONE***<text>*^**KD**

or

>   EDIT/Other/Footnote/endnote.../**E**
>   *<text>*^**KD**

To insert a footnote into your document:

>   ^**ONF***<text>*^**KD**

or

>   EDIT/Other/Footnote/endnote.../**F**
>   *<text>*^**KD**

To view or edit an annotation, comment, endnote, or footnote, place cursor on the note entry, then:

>   ^**OND**

or

>   EDIT/Other/Footnote/endnote.../**D**

To convert one type of note to another, place cursor on the note entry, then:

>   ^**ONV**

or

EDIT/Other/Footnote/endnote.../**V**

To realign notes to new margin settings:

^ONU

or

EDIT/Other/Footnote/endnote.../**U**

To find the next note in your document:

^ONG

or

EDIT/Other/Footnote/endnote.../**G**

To check the spelling of notes:

^ONL

or

EDIT/Other/Footnote/endnote.../**L**

To specify sequencing style and starting symbol for endnotes:

.E# [**A**] [**1**] [*****]

To specify sequencing style and starting symbol for footnotes:

.F# [**A**] [**1**] [*****]

To print endnotes in a location other than the end of the file:

.PE

To convert note types at print time (and resequence them, if applicable):

.CV *x* >*y*

where *x* is the first letter of the note type to be converted and *y* is the first letter of the note type to which they will be converted when printed.

USAGE

You can insert five types of notes into a file: annotations, comments, endnotes, footnotes, and index entries. Comments and index entries are discussed separately under the headings **Comments** and **Index**; see these sections for details. *Annotations* are notes printed at the bottom of the page on which they appear. You can select any character (such as an asterisk) to mark the sentence to which they refer. They are not numbered. *Endnotes* are numbered notes printed at the end of a document or after the **.PE** command. *Footnotes* are also numbered notes but they are printed at the foot of the page, under a line or row of dashes 20 characters long. If a footnote is longer than three lines, the fourth and succeeding lines are carried over to the bottom of the next page.

To create a note, first press **^ON** or select **Other/Footnote/endnote...** from the EDIT pull-down menu. The Notes menu will appear. Next, select the type of note you want to create. To create an annotation, press **A**. The ANNOTATION MARK dialog box will appear. Type the character or characters with which you want to mark the annotation here, and then press ⏎, **^K**, or **F10**. A new window appears at the bottom of the screen beginning with the annotation mark you selected in brighter type or in a different color. Type in the annotation, and then press **^KD** to close the window. If you have display set to on (**^OD**), a tag displays the first words of the annotation in bright text or in a different color and enclosed in square brackets, like this:

[Source: Gov't P]

To view the entire annotation or edit it, position the cursor on the tag and press **^OND**. You can then use the standard editing commands to modify the annotation. To close the annotation window without saving changes, press **^KQ**. To close the annotation window and save changes, press **^KD**.

To create an endnote or footnote, press **^ON** and then press either **E** or **F**, respectively. You will not be prompted to select a type of mark, as with an annotation; a new window will be opened directly. Unless you have selected a different sequencing method, a number will appear in bright text or in a different color. Type in the endnote or footnote. Press ^**KD** to close the note window. A tag will appear as described above. Endnotes and footnotes are edited in the same manner as annotations.

To convert one type of note to another, position the cursor on the note's tag or symbol and press ^**ONV**. Select the appropriate letter for the type of note to which the selected note should be converted (**A** for annotation, **C** for comment, **E** for endnote, or **F** for footnote). If you want to convert all notes of one type to another type at print time, use the dot command **.CV**, as described above.

You can sequence endnotes and footnotes with numbers, letters, or asterisks. The default system uses numbers. You can change the default by inserting the command **.E#** (for endnotes) or **.F#** (for footnotes) followed by **A** for alphabetical, **1** for numeric, or ***** for asterisks. If you don't want to start with 1, A, or *, you can specify a higher number, letter, or larger number of asterisks here.

To print endnotes elsewhere than at the end of the file, insert the command **.PE** at the place where you want them to print. To go to the next note in your file, press ^**ONG**. To spell check your notes, press ^**ONL**. To realign notes after editing or changing margins, press ^**ONU**. To delete a note, delete its number, letter, or mark, or, if control codes are displayed, you can delete the tags that are visible. You can restore a deleted note using ^**U**.

You can change many of the default settings for footnotes and endnotes in WSCHANGE, WordStar's customization program. See **Appendix A** for more information.

Open a Document

See **Document Mode, Nondocument Mode, Speed Write**.

Overprint Character

The following command allows you to print one character over another, if your printer is capable of it.

RELEASE

4 and 5

KEY SEQUENCE

*<first character >***^PH***<second character >*

USAGE

Overprinting characters is useful for printing foreign expressions that contain diacritical marks over individual letters, such as the tilde (~) in *año nuevo* or the circumflex (^) in *raison d'être*. To print one character over another, type one of them (it doesn't matter which one comes first), and then press **^PH**. If you have codes set to display (**^OD**), the code **^H** will appear after the first character. Now type the second character. Although the two characters will not occupy the same position on the screen, notice that the column position on the status line is the same for both characters because they will in fact appear in the same location when printed.

Many foreign characters that can be created using the overprint character command are also available as graphics characters; see the **Graphics Characters** entry for more details.

Not all printers are capable of using the overprint character feature; consult your printer documentation for more information.

SEE ALSO

Graphics Characters

Overprint Line

Overprint Line

The following command allows you to print one line over another.

RELEASE

4 and 5

KEY SEQUENCE

<first line >^**P**↵
<second line >

USAGE ═══════════

You can use this feature to create graphic effects, such as printed type over a shaded bar. To print one line over another, type one line (it doesn't matter which one comes first), then press ^P↵, but don't let the line wrap. A dash (–) will appear in the flag column. Now type the second line, being careful to insert a hard return (↵) at the end of it so that a less-than symbol (<) appears in the flag column. Although both lines will not occupy the same line on the screen, notice that the line number on the status line is the same for both lines because they will in fact appear one on top of the other when printed.

SEE ALSO ═══════════

Graphics Characters

Overprint Characters

Page Breaks

These commands allow you to cause a new page to begin in your document.

RELEASE

4 and 5

KEY SEQUENCE

See individual sections.

USAGE

WordStar normally inserts soft page breaks automatically, indicated on the Edit screen by a line or a row of dashes across the screen ending with a **P** in the flag column. These breaks are based on your margin and page length settings, and they will change any time you add more lines of text or alter the margin settings. If you want to keep certain lines together, prevent inadvertently awkward page breaks, or start a specific section of your document on a new page, use the following commands.

Conditional Page Breaks

The following commands will insert page breaks when certain criteria are met.

KEY SEQUENCE ═══════════════════════

To insert a conditional page break:

.CP *n*

where *n* is the number of lines following the dot command to be kept on the same page.

To insert a conditional page break of 3 lines (in Release 5 only):

EDIT/Layout/Conditional new page...

USAGE ═══════════════════════

Conditional page breaks can be used to keep sections of text together and prevent them from being printed over two pages. These page breaks can be inserted into the text in a location where the text would logically be separated, such as between paragraphs or headings. To issue a conditional page break, insert the command **.CP** immediately preceding the text you do not want to be split over two pages, followed by the number of lines in that section of text. If during the process of editing a page break should occur within the designated lines following the conditional page break command, a new page will start at the location of the command instead of in the middle of the section of text you want on the same page.

Hard Page Breaks

The following commands will insert hard page breaks where they occur in the document.

KEY SEQUENCE ═══════════════════════

To insert a hard page break:

.PA

or (in Release 5 only):

EDIT/Layout/New page

USAGE

Hard page breaks can be used whenever you want to start a specific section of text on a new page. (They must also occur at the end of master documents in merge printing). A new page will then begin immediately following the dot command, despite any added lines or changes to your margin settings. To issue a hard page break, insert the command **.PA** on a line where you want the new page to begin and press ⏎. You can also position your cursor at the location of the desired page break and select **New Page** from the EDIT/Layout menu in Release 5; the page break dot command **.PA** and ⏎ will be inserted into the text at that location. On the line following the dot command, a line or a row of dashes followed by a **P** in the flag column indicates you are on a new page. To start a new page from the middle of a line, see **Form Feed**.

SEE ALSO

Form Feed

Merge Printing

Page Length

The following commands allow you to set the page length of your document.

| RELEASE | ≣≣≣≣≣≣≣≣≣
|---|

4 and 5

| KEY SEQUENCE | ≣≣≣≣≣≣≣≣≣
|---|

To set the page length of a document using lines as a unit of measurement:

.PL *n*

where *n* is the total number of lines on the page.

To set the page length of a document using inches as a unit of measurement (in Release 5 only):

.PL *n.nn"*

or

^OL
[*select* Page length]
n.nn
^K [*or* **F10**]

or

EDIT/Layout/Margins and tabs.../
[*select* Page length]
n.nn
^K [*or* **F10**]

where *n.nn* is the total length of the page in inches.

| USAGE | ≣≣≣≣≣≣≣≣≣
|---|

The page length command can be used to allow you to print on different sizes of paper. The default length is 11 in. or 66 lines, if you are using the default line height. (If you change the line height, page length settings using lines as a unit of measurement will be affected accordingly.) To change the page length to legal-size paper (14 in.), insert the dot command **.PL 84** (for the default line height setting) or **.PL 14.00"** at the top of the page. Inches can be used as a unit of measurement only in Release 5. Note that the page length equals the number of lines of text plus top and bottom margins.

SEE ALSO

Line Height

Margins

Page Numbering

The following commands govern page numbering.

RELEASE

4 and 5

KEY SEQUENCE

To omit page numbering:

.OP

or (in Release 5 only):

EDIT/Layout/Omit page numbering

To turn page numbering back on after a **.OP** command:

.PG

To print the page number in a specific column:

.PC *n*

where *n* is the column in which the page number will appear when printed.

To print the page number at a specific distance from the left margin using inches as a unit of measurement (in Release 5 only):

.PC *n.nn"*

where *n.nn* is the distance in inches from the left margin.

To specify the page number:

.PN *n*

where *n* is the new page number.

USAGE

WordStar normally prints consecutive page numbers at the bottom of each page of a document. To turn this feature off, insert a **.OP** command at the top of the page, either by typing it or, in Release 5, by selecting **Omit page numbering** from the EDIT/Layout pull-down menu. If you want to put the page number in a different location on the page, you can position the page number somewhere other than the center of the bottom line by using **.PC** and then selecting either a new column number or a new distance in inches from the left margin (if you have Release 5). If you want to place the page number at the top of the page or you are using footers, see the entries on **Footers** or **Headers**.

To restart page numbering after a .OP command, insert the command **.PG** at the top of the page where you want page numbering to begin again.

To start page numbering at a number other than one, or to restart page numbering within a document, use the **.PN** command followed by the number with which you want page numbering to begin. The status line will accurately reflect this relative page number setting while you are editing. The merge printing, printing, and Go to page functions will also recognize these new page numbers rather than the literal (that is, absolute) page numbers of a document.

SEE ALSO

Merge Print

Print

Page Offset

The following commands allow you to adjust the margin between the left edge of your paper and column 1 on your screen.

RELEASE

4 and 5

KEY SEQUENCE

To set the page offset using columns as a unit of measurement:

.PO *n*

where *n* is the number of columns of margin from the left edge of the paper to column 1.

To set the page offset using inches as a unit of measurement (in Release 5 only):

.**PO** *n.nn"*

where *n.nn* is the number of inches of margin from the left edge of the paper to column 1.

To set the page offset for even pages only (in Release 5):

.**POE** *n.nn"*

or

EDIT/Layout/Margins and tabs.../
[*select* Even page offset]
n.nn ^**K** [*or* **F10**]

where *n.nn* is the number of inches of margin from the left edge of the paper to column 1.

To set the page offset for odd pages only (in Release 5):

.**POO** *n.nn"*

or

EDIT/Layout/Margins and tabs.../
[*select* Odd page offset]
n.nn ^**K** [*or* **F10**]

where *n.nn* is the number of inches of margin from the left edge of the paper to column 1.

| USAGE |

To set the page offset in Release 4, insert the dot command .**PO** followed by the number of columns of margin you want between the left edge of the paper and column 1. The default value is 8 columns, or .8 in. Note that this shifts all the margin and tab settings relative to the left edge of the paper, not just the left margin. That is, if you set the page offset to 15 (or 1.5 in.), then column 1 would start printing 1.5 in. from the left edge of the page. This means you must adjust your right and left margins accordingly, especially your right margin, if you don't want text to print off the right side of the page.

Page offset behaves much the same way in Release 5 except that you can set the offset in inches. You can also have different page offset settings for odd- and even-numbered pages, a useful feature if you are binding your document like a book and want to control the space from the binding to the beginning of text. If you use the **Margins and tabs** selection from the EDIT/Layout pull-down menu, you cannot select a uniform page offset for both even and odd pages except by entering the same value for both options in the dialog box.

Page Preview

The following commands allow you to view your current document much as it will appear on paper.

RELEASE

4 and 5

KEY SEQUENCE

See individual sections.

USAGE

Page Preview differs substantially between releases; its functions have been greatly expanded in Release 5. See the appropriate sections for the release you are using.

Page Preview, Release 4

The following command allows you to suppress all formatting codes.

KEY SEQUENCE

To switch to and from Page Preview:

^OP

USAGE

To turn Page Preview on or off, press **^OP**. When you turn the preview feature on, the display of all control codes and dot commands will be suppressed so that you can see your page layout without these distractions. This feature is especially useful if you have many formatting commands but you just want to read your text on the screen. When you turn the preview feature on, the words

Prtect Preview

appear in the status line, indicating that you are in both preview mode and protected mode. In protected mode you cannot edit text. If you try to type any text or do anything but move the cursor, you will hear a beep. To return to the Edit screen, simply press **^OP** once more.

Page Preview, Release 5

If you have a graphics monitor, these commands allow you to view your document exactly as it will appear on paper.

KEY SEQUENCE

To switch to and from Page Preview:

^OP

or

EDIT/Layout/Page Preview

To switch to and from currently displayed page:

Alt-1

To switch to and from the original page:

Alt-2

USAGE

Page Preview is a powerful feature, with several of its own
menus. You must have a monitor capable of displaying
graphics to use it, such as a CGA (Color Graphics Adapter)
monitor, a Hercules-type monochrome monitor, or an EGA
(Enhanced Graphics Adapter). To invoke this feature, either
press **^OP**, or select **Page Preview** from the EDIT/Layout
pull-down menu. You can also switch between the same section of the document in the preview and edit screens by
typing **Alt-1**. Pressing **Alt-2** returns you to the original page
you were editing when you went into preview.

Like the Opening screen, Page Preview displays a menu
bar that is activated by pressing the first letter of the menu.
The following lists the menus and the commands that they
activate. The key you press to activate the menu or command
is printed in boldface type.

MENU	COMMAND
Goto	Specified page ...
	First page
	Last page
	Next page
	Previous page
View	Entire page
	Facing pages
	Multiple pages
	Thumbnail display
	2x zoom
	4x zoom
	Adjust window ...
Options	Automatic scan
	Scan range ...
	Grid display On/Off
Return to Editing	Original page
	Current page

Paragraph Alignment

See **Align Paragraphs**.

Paragraph Margins

The following commands allow you to change what Word-Star calls the *paragraph margin,* meaning the default indent of paragraphs in your document. (You can also change it using an embedded ruler line. See **Ruler Line** for more information on this method.)

RELEASE

4 and 5

KEY SEQUENCE

To set the paragraph margin by specifying a column number:

.PM [**+**] *n*

where *n* is the column number of the paragraph margin. If the plus symbol is included (in Release 5 only), succeeding paragraphs will be indented *n* columns beyond the previous paragraph indent.

To set the paragraph margin to column 6:

^F7 *or* **.PM6**

To set the paragraph margin using inches as a unit of measurement (in Release 5 only):

.PM [**+**] *n.nn"*

or

^OL
[Select Paragraph option]
n.nn **^K** [*or* **F10**]

or

> EDIT/Layout/Margins and tabs...
> [Select Paragraph option]
> *n.nn* ^K [*or* **F10**]

where *n.nn* is the distance in inches from column 1. If the plus
symbol is included (in Release 5 only), succeeding paragraphs
will be indented *n.nn* in. beyond the previous paragraph indent.

USAGE

To set the paragraph margin (or indent) within a document
using columns as a unit of measurement, insert the dot command **.PM** followed by the column number designating the
paragraph margin. The letter **P** will appear on the ruler line
at that column whenever your cursor moves below the
line containing the **.PM** command, and the first line of any
paragraph following the command will begin at the
new paragraph margin; you don't have to press **Tab**. The ➤
symbol appears, indicating the indent. The successive lines
will begin at the left margin. If you save the document and
edit it later, this paragraph margin setting will be preserved
until you delete it. WordStar provides the function key command ^F7 to insert the most common paragraph margin of
.PM6 (indented one tab stop on the default ruler line).

To set the paragraph margin using inches as a unit of
measurement, either insert the dot command **.PM** followed
by the distance in inches and the inch symbol ("), or access
the MARGINS & TABS dialog box by pressing ^OL or selecting **Margins and tabs...** from the EDIT/Layout pull-down
menu, use the Tab key twice to reach the paragraph margin
option, and then type in the new margin number expressed
in inches and press ^K or F10. (You needn't type the " symbol using this method.) If you use the MARGINS & TABS
dialog box, the **.PM** dot command as well as some other margin commands, such as the header margin, will appear in
your document, using the current settings.

In Release 5, you can also use this command to indent paragraphs a specific amount more than the previous one by placing a plus symbol (+) immediately after the dot command and before specifying the size of that indent. For example, if you have previously set the paragraph margin as **.PM6**, which would create an indent at column 6, inserting the dot command **.PM+5** would indent the following paragraphs to column 11.

Several of WordStar Release 5's predefined ruler lines use a paragraph margin, and you can also insert a paragraph margin into your own ruler lines. See the **Ruler Line** entry for more details.

Paragraph Numbering

The following commands allow you to number your paragraphs.

RELEASE

5 only

KEY SEQUENCE

To insert a paragraph number:

^OZ [specify level] ↵

or

EDIT/Layout/Paragraph numbering...
[specify level] ↵

To specify number and/or numbering system:

.P# *<n.n.n... etc.>,<level1.level2.level3 >*

where *n.n.n...* is the number with which to begin the paragraph sequence and *level1*, and so on, are the numbering styles for the various levels using the codes described below:

CODE	MEANING
9	Arabic numerals
I	Uppercase roman numerals
i	Lowercase roman numerals
Z	Uppercase letters
z	Lowercase letters

USAGE

To number a paragraph, position your cursor at the place where you want the number to appear, and then press **^OZ** or select **Paragraph numbering...** from the EDIT/Layout pull-down menu. A screen will appear showing you the next paragraph number. If you want to change the level, use ← or **^S** to move up a level and → or **^D** to move down a level. Then press ↵ to accept the number. The Edit screen will return with a highlighted tag numbering your paragraph.

For instance, if you have just finished typing paragraph 2.2 and you want the next paragraph to be subordinately numbered 2.2.1 (instead of 2.3), press → or **^D** at the prompt, and the number **2.2.1** appears on the screen. Press ↵ to accept the option, and the tag **2.2.1** will appear at your cursor position. To remove a paragraph number, simply delete the tag using one of the standard deletion commands such as **^G** or **Del**.

If you delete or insert new paragraph tags, WordStar automatically renumbers them for you.

WordStar starts paragraph numbering beginning with one and using numerals of up to eight levels. If you want to start at a new number, use the dot command **.P#** followed by the new number. You can specify whether you want to use roman numerals or letters in your paragraph numbering style at the same time. Type a comma after the new paragraph number if you are renumbering, and then use the codes listed in the table above, separating the levels by periods. You can use any combination of codes you like. For instance, if you want your paragraphs to be numbered in a standard outline sequence, starting with uppercase roman numerals, then uppercase letters, then arabic numerals, type

.P# *n*, **I.Z.9**

where *n* is the new starting number.

You can also add punctuation in this command—for example, brackets to enclose your paragraph number:

.P# *n*, **[I.Z.9]**

You can change the default numbering style using WSCHANGE. See Appendix A for more details.

Path

See **Drive.**

Phantom Rubout and Phantom Space

These commands allow you to print special characters on some printers.

RELEASE

4 and 5

KEY SEQUENCE

To insert a phantom rubout character:

^PG

To insert a phantom space character:

^PF

USAGE

These commands apply primarily to certain daisy-wheel printers that have on their print wheels one or two characters not found in the standard character set. Insert the codes in a test file and print them to see what character your printer produces. To insert a phantom rubout or space character, press **^PG** or **^PF**, respectively. If your code display is on, ^G will appear for phantom rubout, and ^F for phantom space. If code display is off, a tilde (~) will appear on-screen to represent the phantom rubout character and a blank space will represent the phantom space character.

Pitch

The following commands allow you to switch between your default pitch and an alternate pitch.

RELEASE ==

4 and 5

KEY SEQUENCE ====================================

To begin printing using an alternate pitch:

^PA

To resume printing in normal pitch:

^PN

USAGE ==

To select the alternate pitch in a document, press **^PA**. The code **^A** (in Release 4) or <ALTERNATE> (in Release 5) will appear in your text if you have codes set to display. To resume normal pitch, press **^PN**. **^N** (in Release 4) or <NORMAL> (in Release 5) will appear if codes are set to display.

For typewriters, the term *pitch* signifies the number of characters per inch, usually either Pica (10 characters per inch) or Elite (12 characters per inch). These terms also apply to daisy-wheel printers and nonproportional fonts in general. Selecting alternate pitch switches from your standard pitch to a preselected alternate. You should experiment to see how this command behaves with your printer.

If you have a daisy-wheel printer and you use the alternate pitch command to change pitch, but you also want to use a different print wheel (with different size type), you must use it in conjunction with the Print Pause command (**^PC**) described in the section by that name so that your printer will pause to allow you to change wheels.

SEE ALSO

Choose Font

Character Width

Place Markers

See **Markers.**

Print

The following commands allow you to send documents to your printer or to a disk file.

RELEASE

4 and 5

KEY SEQUENCE

To print a file from the Classic Opening menu:

P *<d:\pathname\filename.ext >*

or (in Release 5 only):

File/Print a file...
<d:\pathname\filename.ext >

To print a file from the Edit screen:

^KP *<d:\pathname\filename.ext >*

or (in Release 5 only):

EDIT/File/Print a file...
<d:\pathname\filename.ext >

To open WordStar and print a file from the DOS prompt in Release 4:

WS *<d:\pathname\filename.ext >* **P**

To open WordStar from DOS, print a file, then exit back to DOS in Release 4:

WS *<d:\pathname\filename.ext >* **PX**

To open WordStar and print a file from the DOS prompt in Release 5:

WS*<d:\pathname\filename.ext >* **/P**

To open WordStar from DOS, print a file, then exit back to DOS in Release 5:

WS*<d:\pathname\filename.ext >* **/P /X**

USAGE

To print a file, press **P** or select **File/Print a file...** (using the Release 5 pull-down menus) from the Classic Opening menu, or press **^KP** or select **EDIT/File/Print a file...** from the Edit screen, first making sure that your printer is connected properly and is online.

In Release 4, enter the name of the document or press ^X
or ↓ to move your cursor into the current directory and highlight the file to be printed. When have selected the file, press
↵. You will be prompted to answer the following questions
before printing (if you want to accept all the default answers
to these questions, press **Esc**):

```
               Number of copies?  [1]
    Pause between pages (Y/N)?  [usually N]
        Use form feeds (Y/N)?  [usually N]
              Starting page?  [first page]
               Ending page?  [last page]
          Nondocument (Y/N)?  [N]
            Name of printer?  [your default printer]
```

The prompts are self-explanatory, except perhaps for the final
two. The information in brackets shows WordStar's general defaults. Check your own installed version to see what
the defaults are with your printer. To accept a default answer,
you can simply press ↵. If you do not want to accept a default
answer, you must answer all the questions above it (using ↵
to accept the default), and then enter the nondefault value for
that item. You can then either press **Esc** to accept the remaining defaults or continue answering the questions until the end.

The Nondocument prompt allows you to print your document without any formatting; any dot commands or merge
variables will be printed as they appear on screen, which can
be useful if you want to examine a complicated document format closely.

The last prompt requires more explanation. If you are using
only one printer and it has been selected in the installation
procedure, you can accept the default printer. If, however,
you are using more than one printer, or you have a laser
printer with different modes (portrait and landscape) and different cartridges, or you want to print to a disk file instead of
a printer, you will have to select the printer. When you come
to the printer selection prompt, a list of possible *printer drivers*
(program routines that communicate with and therefore *drive*
specific printers) appears at the bottom of your screen. You
can either accept the default, type in another name from the

list, or use the cursor keys to select a driver. You can select any printer or printer configuration you have connected to your computer, as well as other special print drivers such as ASCII, which prints an ASCII text file to disk. More information on these special print drivers is included in the table below. (See **ASCII Conversion** for more information.)

In Release 5, the PRINT dialog box will appear when you invoke one of the printing commands listed above. If you have already selected a file during your current editing session, that file will appear after the File prompt. Otherwise, the word "none" will appear. Enter the name of the document or press **^X** or ↓ to move your cursor into the current directory and highlight the file to be printed. When you have selected the file, press ↵. You can then move through the dialog box using the **Tab** key or **^I** and change any of the options available. (If you want to accept all the default answers to these questions, just press **^K** or **F10**.)

The first option after the file name is Page numbers. You can select any page or series of pages to print (the default value is A, for all pages). To print pages 1 through 4, for example, you would type **1-4**. To print pages 5, 8, and 16, you would type **5,8,16**. You can also combine these two methods; typing **1-3,5,8,16** would print pages 1, 2, 3, 5, 8, and 16. The next option is All/even/odd pages. The default is **A**, for all. Press **E** to print even pages only or **O** to print odd pages only. These even and odd selections can be used to print on both sides of a sheet of paper, as in a book, by printing odd pages first, turning them over, and then printing the even pages on the other side.

The next prompt is the printer name. Notice that when you reach this prompt, the file directory disappears and a list of printers appears in its place, with the printer that is currently selected both after the Printer name prompt and in parentheses above the list of printers. You can also designate a printer using the change printer command (**^P?**) within your document (see the **Change Printer** entry), in which case this step is not necessary. If you are using only one printer and it has been selected in the installation procedure or by using PRCHANGE (see Appendix A), you can generally accept the default printer here by pressing ↵, **Tab**, or **^I**. If, however, you

are using more than one printer, or you have a laser printer
with different modes (portrait and landscape) and different
cartridges, or you want to print to a disk file instead of a
printer, you will have to select the printer. You can either accept the default, type in another name from the list , or use
the cursor keys to select a driver. You can select any printer
or printer configuration you have connected to your computer, as well as several special print drivers that print versions of your file to disk. A list of these special print drivers
and their uses follows.

NAME	OUTPUT FILE NAME	FUNCTION
ASC256	ASC256.WS	Produces an ASCII text file including the IBM graphic characters (such as the box-drawing characters and foreign currency symbols).
ASCII	ASCII.WS	Produces a standard ASCII text file, removing all printing effects such as boldface and underline and dot commands, inserting hard carriage returns on every line. Best for transferring to other programs or files not requiring reediting. Useful for previewing the final appearance of document and the location on the page of headers, footers, and notes.

PREVIEW (Release 5) *or* PRVIEW (Release 4)	PREVIEW.WS PRWIEW.WS	Produces a file showing location of all headers and footers, (and inserted data if merge printing); inserts .PL at beginning of file for proper display of page breaks as they will appear when printed. Also inserts hard carriage returns on every line.
TYPEWR	(no disk file)	Prints as you type directly from the Edit screen like a typewriter. Useful for single envelopes and mailing labels.
WS4	WS4.WS	Produces a file in WordStar Release 4 format.
XTRACT	XTRACT.WS	Produces a file similar to PREVIEW, but does not show headers, footers, or page breaks. Uses soft carriage returns, allowing for some editing capabilities.

(If you don't want your new disk file to have the default file name listed above, assign it a different one at the Redirect output to prompt.)

The next option is Pause between pages. Answer yes if you are feeding single sheets into your printer by hand. The next option asks whether you want to use form feeds. See your printer documentation and test your printer to determine whether to answer yes or no to this question.

The Nondocument prompt allows you to print your document without any formatting or simply to print out nondocument files.

The Number of copies option allows you to print more than one copy of a document. If you elect to print more than one, the printer will print all pages of the first copy, then all the pages of the second copy, and so on.

The Redirect output to option allows you specify a file name when you are printing to disk instead of to the printer, as described above. You can also use this option to print a file to disk so that you can print it from another computer (that need not have WordStar). Select the printer you intend to use, and then move to the Redirect output to option and assign a name to the file. You can then print the file using the DOS command COPY in the following format:

D>COPY *<d:\pathname\filename.ext >* *<port >*

The *port* specification is the output port (such as LPT1 or COM1) that is connected to your printer.

Once you have selected all the options necessary to print your file, exit the dialog box by pressing **^K** or **F10**.

With either release, once the file begins to print, you will see the message Printing on the status line (or on the top line if you are in the Classic Opening menu). If you want to maximize print speed and don't need to be editing or performing other operations concurrently with the print operation, select again the key sequence to print a file. The PRINTING dialog box or menu will appear on your screen. The options are described below.

COMMAND	FUNCTION
P	Causes the print operation to stop temporarily
C	Resumes print operation after pause
B	Returns to concurrent printing (printing in the background)
^U	Cancels printing

F   Prints at full speed with the PRINTING
           dialog box or menu and allows no other
           operations to occur

Change Printer

This command allows you to select a printer for a specific file.

RELEASE

5 only

KEY SEQUENCE

^P? *<printer name >* **^K** [*or* **F10**]

USAGE

To insert a tag to specify a new printer in a file, press **^P?**. The
CHANGE PRINTER dialog box appears, along with a list of
possible choices of printers. Select the new printer either by
typing in the name or by highlighting it using the cursor keys.
Then press **^K** or **F10** to accept the choice.

SEE ALSO

ASCII Conversion

Command File

Merge Print

Print Pause

Print Pause

The following command allows you to make your printer pause so that you can change ribbons, print wheels, or cartridges in a specific place in your document.

RELEASE

4 and 5

KEY SEQUENCE

To insert a print pause into your document:

^PC

To resume printing after a pause during background printing in Release 4 from the Opening menu:

PC

or from the Edit screen:

^KPC

To resume printing after a pause during background printing in Release 5 from the Opening menu:

PC

or

File/Print a file.../**C**

or, from the Edit screen:

^KPC

or

EDIT/File/Print a file.../**C**

To resume printing when background printing is turned off from the Opening menu (either release):

C

USAGE	

To insert a print pause command into a document, press **^PC** at the point where you want the pause to occur. The code **^C** will appear in your document if you have codes set to display. The purpose of this command is to allow you to change some element in your printer at a specific location in your document. It is necessary when you want to change fonts and you need to switch print wheels or cartridges to do so.

When you print a document that contains print pause codes, your printer will stop when it reaches the code. If you have Release 5, you will also hear a beep. At this point, make the necessary changes to your printer, making sure that it is online before you proceed to the next step. If you are in background printing mode, the message

Print Wait

will appear on the status line. You must then access the Printing menu to continue printing. If you are using Release 4, press **P** from the Opening menu or **^KP** from the Edit screen. If you are using Release 5, press **P** or select **File/Print a file...** from the Opening menu or press **^KP** or select **EDIT/File/Print a file...** from the Edit screen. The Printing menu will now appear. If you are not using background printing, the Printing menu will already be present. In either case, the following message will be displayed beneath it:

Printing paused. Press C to continue or P to pause again at next page.

This message may at first be misleading. WordStar uses the same message for pausing between pages (an option at print time), and therefore the second part of the message is irrelevant. Press **C** to continue, unless you have also selected the **Pause between pages** option to insert individual sheets of paper into your printer manually in addition to the print pause command, in which case you should press **P**.

SEE ALSO

Print

Proportional Spacing

The following command turns proportional fonts on and off.

RELEASE

4 and 5

KEY SEQUENCE

.PS ON/OFF

USAGE

Proportional fonts add space around characters, taking into account the width of each character when printed (an *m* takes up more space than an *i*, for instance) and thereby providing the appearance of professional typesetting.

Nonproportional fonts give the same amount of space to every character, regardless of its individual width.

If you have Release 5, you may find it easier to use the choose font command (^P=) to choose between proportionally and nonproportionally spaced fonts. If you have only a few fonts available or if you have Release 4, use the dot command **.PS ON** to turn proportional spacing on. (Unless you change your printer defaults in WSCHANGE, your primary or default font is probably nonproportional.) To turn proportional spacing off, use the command **.PS OFF**. Note that this command is useful only if you have both types of fonts on your printer; you cannot make a nonproportional font proportional or vice versa.

SEE ALSO

Choose Font

Column Alignment

Protect/Unprotect

The following commands allow you to protect files from editing or deletion or to remove that protection.

RELEASE

4 and 5

To protect or unprotect a file from the Classic Opening menu:

C *<d:\pathname\filename.ext >*

from the pull-down Opening menu:

File/Protect/unprotect a file...
<d:\pathname\filename.ext >

It should be made clear that protecting a file in WordStar *in no way makes it confidential.* The protection command is a useful tool to keep important documents from being altered by accident, but anyone using your computer can *unprotect* the file. If you want to make something confidential, you will need to investigate one of the commercially available third-party security programs.

To protect a file from editing or deletion from within WordStar, press **C**, or, if you are using Release 5 pull-down menus, select **File/Protect/unprotect a file...** from the Opening menu. Next, enter the name of the file you want to protect and press ↵. If the file is not protected, you will see the message

This file is currently not protected. Protect it? (Y/N)

in Release 5 and a similar message in Release 4. If you are sure you want to protect it, press **Y**. Once you have protected a file, you cannot alter it or delete it, although you can continue to open the document, move around in it, and view it as you normally would. If you do, you will see the message

Prtect

on the status line. If you try to add or delete text or change the formatting, you will hear a beep, and nothing will happen. To exit a protected file, you must use the quit and abandon command **^KQ**. If you try to delete a protected file from within WordStar, the message

Can't delete a protected file.
Press **Esc** to continue.

appears on your screen. If you try to delete the file from DOS using DEL or ERASE, you will receive the message

Access denied

To unprotect a file, just perform the same operation as above, specifying the file you want to unprotect. After you select the file you will see this prompt (or a similar one in Release 4)

This file is currently protected. Unprotect it? (Y/N)

Answer **Y** to unprotect the file.

You can still copy a file or mark a block and copy it to a separate file when the file is protected, but you cannot rename the file.

Quit WordStar

See **Exit WordStar**.

RAM Usage

The following commands allow you to see how much of your computer's memory is being used and what it is being used for.

RELEASE

4 and 5

KEY SEQUENCE

From the Classic Opening menu:

?

or from the pull-down Opening menu:

Other/Display RAM usage...

USAGE

To see how much of your computer's RAM (Random Access Memory) is being used by WordStar and in what way, press **?** at the Classic Opening menu (note that the **?** is not listed as one of the options) or, if you are using Release 5 pull-down menus, select **Other/Display RAM usage...** from the Opening menu. You will then see a list showing how much memory WordStar is using at the time, something like the one below (the figures will vary, especially for the Text and data field):

Memory Usage...

WordStar   139k
Text and data   127k

Messages	24k
Printing	46k
Spelling	87k
Thesaurus	Shared
Hyphenation	Shared
Total	423k
Unused memory	96k

Press **Esc** to continue.

If you have Release 4, the Spelling and Thesaurus fields are replaced by the CorrectStar field, and there are no fields showing the hyphenation or amount of unused memory. In Release 5, it should be noted that the Unused memory field has already calculated the amount being used by DOS and any TSR (terminate-and-stay-resident) programs, such as SideKick or Inset, loaded before entering WordStar, that are allocated memory because they run concurrently with WordStar.

You can get more information about how much memory is free as well as your current disk storage capacity by using DOS commands with the **Run a DOS command** option. See that section for more details.

SEE ALSO

Run a DOS Command

Read Block

See **Block Operations**.

Read File

See **Block Operations.**

Rename

The following commands allow you to rename a file.

RELEASE

4 and 5

KEY SEQUENCE

To rename a file from the Classic Opening menu:

E *<old filename >* ↵
<new filename > ↵

or from the pull-down Opening menu:

File/Rename a file...
<old filename > ↵
<new filename > ↵

To rename a file from the Edit screen:

^KE *<old filename >* ↵
<new filename > ↵

or (in Release 5 only):

> EDIT/File/Rename a file...
> <*old filename* > ⏎
> <*new filename* > ⏎

| USAGE | ===================

To rename a file from the Classic Opening menu, press **E**, or select **File/Rename a file...** if you are using the Release 5 pull-down menus.

In Release 4, you will see the message:

> Document to be renamed?

Enter the name of the document or press **^X** or ↓ to move your cursor into the current directory and highlight the file to be renamed. When you have selected the file, press ⏎. You will see the message:

> What do you want its new name to be?

Enter the new name for the document and then press ⏎.

In Release 5, after selecting the Rename command you will see the RENAME dialog box. The name of the last renamed file (if there was one in the current editing session) will appear after the prompt

> Current name

Enter the name of the file you want to rename (or select it from the current directory by pressing **^X** or ↓ and then highlighting the desired file) and then press ⏎, **Tab**, or **^I**. The cursor will move down to the next prompt:

> New name

Type in the new name here, and then press ⏎, **^K**, or **F10**.

Both releases have certain limitations to the rename command. You cannot use it to move a file from one drive to another by specifying a new drive letter for the new name. And although you *can* rename files to move them from one directory to another, you cannot rename the file you are currently working on.

Repeat

The following command allows you to repeat a single character or a single letter control command.

RELEASE

4 and 5

KEY SEQUENCE

^QQ *<character or command>* n

where *n* is a number 0–9, 0 being the fastest setting and 9 the slowest.

USAGE

To repeat a character or a single letter control command (such as **^C** to scroll a page at a time), press **^QQ** followed by the character or control code you want to be repeated. If you want the repeat operation to proceed swiftly, type **0** or some other low number; if you want the repeat operation to occur slowly, press **9**. You can press numbers anytime during the repeat operation to adjust the speed. If you use the repeat command later, it will operate at the speed you last selected until you specify otherwise. To stop the repeat operation, press the

Spacebar. (You can in fact press any key except one of the numbers to stop a repeat if you make a mistake, like repeating a delete operation by accident.)

TIP

Although the repeat command is limited to repeating a single character, you can use it to repeat larger portions of text as long as the block of text is small enough to unerase. Delete the text to be repeated, using whichever single deletion command can delete the text, and then press ^QQ^U. WordStar will repeat the Unerase operation, thus copying the "unerased" section of text over and over again in your document.

Replace

The following commands find one or more occurrences of a specified text string within a document and replace it with another one.

RELEASE

4 and 5

KEY SEQUENCE

To replace a specific text string:

^**QA**<old text >↵
<new text >↵
<options >↵

or

^F2 *<old text >*↵
<new text >↵
<options >↵

or (in Release 5 only):

EDIT/Go to/Find and replace text...
<old text >↵
<new text >↵
<options >↵

To repeat the last search and replace:

^L

or

^F3

or (in Release 5 only):

EDIT/Go to/Repeat previous find/replace

USAGE

To replace a specific string of text within a document, press
^QA or **^F2** or, in Release 5 only, select **Find and replace text...**
from the EDIT/Go to pull-down menu. Type in the string of
characters you want to replace. If you are looking for something
similar to what you sought in a previous search, pressing **^R** will insert the string of characters from the last **^QF**
(Find) or **^QA** operation. You can use the normal editing keys
to change or delete characters. To search for codes that appear
in the text, you must press **^P** before the control code in order
for it to be understood. For instance, to find boldface codes,
you must press **^P^B**, not just **^B**. To find a hard carriage
return (usually the end of a paragraph), look for the code
^P^M^P^J. You can use the question mark (**?**) as a wild-card
character to represent any character if you later select the wild-
card option. For instance, if you want to replace all five-letter

words beginning with *qu*, you would type **qu???** as your text string. You cannot use the wild-card option in the replacement section, however; WordStar would insert question marks as replacement text.

The text string to search for can be up to 65 characters long (including codes). When you are finished typing it in, press ↵ and the cursor moves down to the Options prompt.

At the Options prompt, you can specify certain aspects of how the search will be performed. Options can be combined in any logical combination. To enter an option, simply press the corresponding letter at the prompt. If you select more than one, type them consecutively in any order but with no spaces between them. The following is a list of options available and a description of their functions.

CODE	FUNCTION
A	Aligns paragraphs where text is replaced.
B	Searches backward through the text toward the beginning of the document from the current cursor position.
G	Searches from the beginning (or end if B is also selected) of the document.
M	(Release 5 only.) Maintains case (upper-, lower-case, or initial capital) of word being replaced.
N	Replaces text without confirmation.
R	Replaces text string throughout the rest of the file.
U	Searches for either uppercase or lowercase occurrences of the characters in the text string.
W	Searches for whole words only.
?	Treats ? characters in the search string as wild-card characters instead of literal question marks.
n	Searches for the *n*th occurrence of the search string.

If you want to repeat a search for the string you last specified, simply press **^L**. This command will repeat either the last Find or Replace operation. If you performed a Replace operation last but want to perform a Find, you must invoke the Find command (**^QF**) and press **^R** to specify previous arguments. Also note that the Repeat Search command does not allow you to change options.

Right Justification

The following commands allow you to turn right justification on and off.

RELEASE

4 and 5

KEY SEQUENCE

To turn right justification on or off in a document:

^OJ

or (in Release 5 only):

EDIT/Layout/Right-justify text

To insert a right justification code within the document:

.OJ ON/OFF

USAGE

With WordStar's default settings, text in word-wrapped paragraphs aligns on the right margin (as well as the left) because spaces are inserted between words until they become flush with the right margin. This is called *right justification*. (In Release 5, the message **RgtJust** also appears on the status line when right justification is in effect.) If you prefer, however, you can have text with only those spaces you type between words; the result will be a *ragged right* margin. To change between these two modes, either press **^OJ** or select **EDIT/Layout/Right-justify text**. Any text you type following this command will reflect the new setting. If you want to change existing text, issue the command and then move your cursor above that paragraph or those paragraphs and press **^B** or **^QU**. The text will realign according to the method you selected.

If you want to have certain sections of text right-justified and others ragged right, or you know you will be editing a document again and want to preserve the same word wrap-style, use the dot command **.OJ** followed by **ON** if you want the text right-justified and **OFF** if you want it ragged right. As with the control command, you must press **^B** or **^QU** to realign existing text if these commands are inserted into existing text.

SEE ALSO

Align Paragraphs

Auto-Align

WordWrap

Ruler Line

The following commands allow you to manipulate horizontal margins and tabs using a ruler line.

RELEASE

4 and 5

KEY SEQUENCE

To embed the current margin and tab settings as a ruler line into a document:

^OO

To embed new margin and tab settings as a ruler line into a document:

.RR*<ruler line characters listed below >*

To embed a preset ruler line into a document (in Release 5 only):

.RR *n*

where *n* is a number 0–9.

To make a ruler line conform to the left and right margins of the current line:

^OF

USAGE

Ruler lines have two functions, as outlined in the section on the ruler line in Part 1. The line under the status line (or the menu bar if you are using the pull-down menus in Release 5) displays the left, right, and paragraph margins, as well as decimal and column tabs. The codes for these margins and tabs are listed below:

L   Left margin

-    Space

!   Tab

\#   Decimal tab (used to align numbers vertically along a column)

P   Paragraph margin

R   Right margin

V   Temporary indent

To insert the current displayed ruler line as a permanent setting within your document, press **^OO**. Anything below that line in your document will follow those settings. A ruler line will be inserted starting with the dot command **.RR** and followed by the current margin and tab settings. If the left margin is set to column 0"– 0.2" (or columns 1, 2, or 3), no **L** symbol will appear because the **.RR** occupies these positions on the screen. It unfortunately follows that left margins of 0.2" or 0.3" (or column 2 or 3) will be eliminated. Use the **.LM** (left margin) command with the appropriate inch measurement or column number following the ruler line to get around this problem.

You can also insert a new ruler line by typing **.RR** followed by the symbols shown above, with the exception of the **V** symbol. This symbol is used only in conjunction with the indent command (**^OG**) to create a temporary indention, and typing it into an embedded ruler line will cause WordStar to indent erratically. Note that if you insert this ruler line above existing text, you must realign the text that follows it by using **^B** or **^QU**.

The remaining symbols function as follows: The hyphen (-) serves as a space or place holder on the ruler line to separate margins and tabs. The exclamation point (!) indicates a standard tab stop. The pound sign (#) indicates a decimal tab stop; this differs from a standard tab stop in that each new character you type will move the preceding text (normally numerals) one space to the left until a decimal point (a period) is typed. The remaining text will appear after the decimal tab. This is particularly useful for columnar lists of numbers. The **P** indicates the paragraph margin, which indents the first line of every paragraph to the corresponding position indicated by the ruler line. The **R** indicates the right margin setting.

In Release 5, you can use ten preset ruler lines by typing **.RR** followed by a number between 0 and 9. The settings provided by WordStar are 0–2 and are described in the table below. Settings 3–9 are reserved for your own customization in WSCHANGE (on the Page Layout submenu of the Word-Star menu).

0 WordStar's default ruler line (left margin 0, standard tabs 0.5 inches apart, and a right margin at 6.5 inches)

1 Indented excerpt format: left and right margins 0.5 inch in from default margins

2 Hanging indent format: first line of each paragraph begins at 0, remaining lines indented 0.5 inch

To set your left and right margins by the indent and width of text on the current line, press **^OF**. This command will not insert an embedded ruler line into your text.

SEE ALSO

Indent

Margins

Paragraph Margins

Tabs

Run a DOS Command

The following commands allow you to run a DOS command without leaving WordStar.

RELEASE ========================

4 and 5

KEY SEQUENCE ========================

To run a DOS command from the Opening menu:

   R *<DOS command >*

or (in Release 5 only):

   Other/Run a DOS command.../*<DOS command >*

To run a DOS command from the Edit screen:

   ^KF *<DOS command >*

or (in Release 5 only):

   EDIT/Other/Run a DOS command.../*<DOS command >*

USAGE ========================

To run a DOS command, use one of the key sequences listed above. The DOS prompt, which is the current drive letter followed by the greater-than symbol (>), appears. Type in the command you want to execute here. When it is finished executing, the following prompt will appear:

   Press any key to return to WordStar.

Press any key and you will be returned to wherever you left WordStar.

There are some limitations to this feature. First, since WordStar is still residing in your computer's memory, you cannot perform a DOS operation that requires a great deal of memory (such as starting another application). Second, you cannot load a TSR (terminate-and-stay-resident) application such as SideKick or WordFinder using this feature because doing so will confuse WordStar's memory allocation routine and "lock up" your computer.

Whenever you use this feature from the Edit screen, be sure to save the file you are working on first, just in case.

Save

The following commands allow you to save files in WordStar.

4 and 5

COMMAND	FUNCTION
^KS *or* **F9** *or* EDIT/File/Save file, resume editing*	Save a file and return to editing
^KD *or* **F10** *or* EDIT/File/Save file, go to Opening screen*	Save and close a file and go to the Opening menu
^KD *or* **F10** *or* EDIT/Win-dow/Close and Save window*	Save and close a window
^PrtSc	Save a file, then print it
^KX *or* **F10** *or* EDIT/File/Save file, exit WordStar*	Save and close a file, then exit WordStar

^KT *<d:\pathname*   Save and name a file
\filename.ext>
or
EDIT/File/Save
and name file
<d:\pathname
*\filename.ext>**

^KQ   Abandon a file without saving
or   changes
EDIT/File/Aban-
don changes*

KQ*   Abandon a window without
or   saving changes
EDIT/Win-
dow/Close and
abandon window*

*Release 5 only

USAGE

There are various ways to save files in WordStar. To save a temporary backup file during editing, press **^KS** or **F9** or select **Save file, resume editing** from the EDIT/File pull-down menu. When you later close the file, you will see a copy of the file in the directory with the extension **.BAK**; this copy will contain the version of the file you made during your last save operation. Before you close the file, WordStar saves temporary copies of your file with the same file name but with the extension **.A** for the last save you initiated and **.B** for the save before that. If your power goes out or you don't close the file properly for some reason, look for the files with these extensions instead of the **.BAK** file—they will contain copies of the file as it appeared during the last two save operations. If you need to use either of these temporary backup files, be sure to rename them before using them to prevent them from being automatically overwritten. You can change the default extensions to some other set of characters in WSCHANGE (see Appendix A).

To save and close a file, press **^KD** or **F10** or select **Save file, go to Opening screen** from the EDIT/File pull-down menu. The file and its **.BAK** backup file, if any, will appear in the directory (unless you have been working on a file that is not in the current drive and/or directory).

To save and close a window, press **^KD** or **F10** or select **Close and save window** from the EDIT/Window pull-down menu. The file in that window will be saved to disk, and you can resume editing in the single remaining window.

If you want to save a file and then print a copy of it, press **^PrtSc**, which will take you to the Print screen in Release 4 and the PRINT dialog box in Release 5. You have access to all print options normally available, but you cannot use this procedure to merge print. If you are using the Speed Write feature in Release 5 and have not yet named your document, you will be prompted to do so before you can go on to the print operation.

To save your document and then exit WordStar to DOS, press **^KX** or select **Save file, exit WordStar** from the EDIT/File pull-down menu.

In Release 5 you can also save and name a file. Press **^KT** or select **Save and name file** from the EDIT/File pull-down menu to name a Speed Write document or rename a document you have already named. You can include a different drive and/or directory name. This command can really be a lifesaver if you have run out of space on a disk and want to save the file somewhere else but you haven't closed the file yet. Just use a different valid drive letter to copy the file to a disk with more room in another disk drive. In Release 4, you can perform the same function by marking your entire document as a block and then using **^KW** to write that block to a new file with a name of your choosing (see **Block Operations**).

To abandon a file and any changes made to it during an editing session, press **^KQ** or select **Abandon changes** from the EDIT/File pull-down menu. If you have not changed the file since you opened it, you will return to the Opening menu.

If you have altered the file, the following prompt will appear (in Release 4 it is worded slightly differently):

Changes have been made. Abandon anyway (Y/N)?

If you are sure you want to abandon all changes (including those that you temporarily saved with ^KS), press **Y**. If you are viewing a document that is in protected mode, you must use this command to exit from the document because Word-Star does not permit you to alter and save protected files.

To abandon and close a window, press ^KD or **F10** or select **Close and abandon window** from the EDIT/Window pull-down menu. You will see the same prompt as shown above. If you press **Y**, the file in that window will be abandoned, and you can resume editing in the single remaining window.

SEE ALSO

Block Operations

Exit

Protect/Unprotect

Scroll

The following commands allow you to scroll the screen up and down within your document.

RELEASE

4 and 5

KEY SEQUENCE	

COMMAND	FUNCTION
^W	One line up
^Z	One line down
^R *or* PgUp	One screenful up
^C *or* PgDn	One screenful down
^QW *n**	Continuously upward, one line at a time
^QZ *n**	Continuously downward, one line at a time
^QQR *n**	Continuously upward, one screen at a time
^QQC *n**	Continuously downward, one screen at a time
Spacebar	Stop continuous scrolling

*n is a number between 0–9; 0 is the fastest, 9 is the slowest

USAGE	

You can scroll through your document in WordStar in several ways. To scroll the screen up in the file (which means the text and cursor move *down*), press **^W**. If the cursor reaches the bottom of the screen, it will remain there as you continue to scroll up. To scroll the screen down in the file (which means the text and cursor move *up*), press **^Z**. If the cursor reaches the top of the screen, it will remain there as you scroll down. To scroll up a full screen, press **^R** or **PgUp**. The cursor will appear in the same relative position on the monitor. To scroll down a full screen, press **^C** or **PgDn**. The cursor will appear in the same relative position.

To scroll up repeatedly a line at a time, press **^QW**. You may adjust the speed at which the scrolling occurs by typing a number in the range 0–9 at this point, 0 being the fastest and 9 being the slowest. To scroll down a line at a time, press **^QZ**.

You can adjust the scrolling speed as with **^QW**. To stop scrolling in either direction, press the Spacebar.

To scroll repeatedly up or down a screen at a time, use the repeat command (**^QQ**) followed by **^R** to scroll up a screen or **^C** to scroll down a screen. The scrolling speed can be adjusted as with the other repeated-scrolling commands. To stop scrolling a screen at a time, press the Spacebar.

SEE ALSO

Cursor Movement

Go To

Repeat

Shorthand

The following commands allow you to generate and execute shorthand macros. For WordStar's predefined macros, see the appropriate entries: **Block Math** under the **Block Operations** entry, **Calculator**, **Date**, and **Time**.

RELEASE

4 and 5

KEY SEQUENCE

To define or edit a shorthand macro:

Esc ? *X <macro description > <command or text string >*

or (in Release 5 only)

EDIT/Other/Shorthand macros...
? X <macro description> <command or text string>

where X is the letter or number (0–9) assigned to a given macro.

To execute a user-defined shorthand macro:

Esc X

or (in Release 5 only):

EDIT/Other/Shorthand macros.../X

where X is the letter or number (0–9) assigned to a given macro.

USAGE

A shorthand *macro* will execute a series of commands or insert a text string into your document, whenever you turn on WordStar's macro feature and type the macro's one-character name. To define a macro, press **Esc** or select **Shorthand macros...** from the EDIT/Other pull-down menu. (Note that you cannot press the alternative key sequence listed to the right of the selection (**Esc**) instead of using the highlight bar in the pull-down menu, because **Esc** is used to exit pull-down menus.) A list of currently defined macros with brief descriptions appears on your screen. Next, press **?** to define a macro. Select a character to represent the macro. The character must be a letter or number (0–9). The nonalphanumeric symbols are reserved for WordStar's predefined macros for inserting the date, time, and results of mathematical calculations into documents.

After selecting a character to represent the macro, you are prompted to provide a description that will be displayed to the right of the character that represents the macro every time the Shorthand menu is accessed. You can ignore the prompt, but if you use many macros, the descriptions will help you keep track of what they do. The description can be up to 50 characters long.

Next, you provide the macro definition. A shorthand macro can consist of any text or command string or combination of text and commands. Type in text exactly as you want it to appear. Type **^P** before any control commands to insert them in macros. For example, to insert the text string **URGENT NOTICE** to appear in boldface type, enclose it within **^P^B** codes. If you want a hard return to appear in your text or command string, press **^PM**. To end a macro definition, press ⏎.

You will be asked to assign a character for another macro; if you want to define only one macro or you have just defined the last one in a list, press ⏎ here. You will be asked whether you want to save changes to disk. If this is a macro you need only for this document, answer **N**; otherwise answer **Y**. The macros are saved in a file called WSSHORT.OVL.

You are limited to a total of 512 bytes of memory for all your shorthand macros; the number of bytes currently available is displayed just above the list of existing macros. You can reduce the amount of memory your macros use by keeping your descriptions short. You can also increase the default memory allocation to more than 512 bytes by using WSCHANGE.

It is also possible to invoke one macro from another macro; this procedure is called *chaining macros*. Type **^P Esc** (which will appear as **^[** on-screen) followed by the character that represents the second macro to be invoked into the definition of the first macro. Using this technique, you can create complex, automated routines activated by only two keystrokes.

SEE ALSO

Block Operations

Calculator

Date

Time

Soft Space Display

The following command allows you to display or hide soft spaces on-screen.

RELEASE

4 and 5

KEY SEQUENCE

^OB

USAGE

Soft spaces are those spaces that you insert between words in WordStar to create a temporary indention, right-justified paragraphs, and so forth, as distinguished from hard spaces that you enter by pressing the Spacebar. Soft spaces are normally invisible, but you can make them appear as a small dot above the line (·). You would do this primarily if you have misalignment or spacing problems and want to see where the soft spaces have been inserted. To do so, press ^OB. To turn soft space display off, press ^OB again. You can change the dot character that is displayed to another one of your choosing with WSCHANGE.

Sort

The following commands allow you to sort lines in a marked block in alphanumeric order.

RELEASE

5 only

KEY SEQUENCE

To sort lines in ascending order:

^KZ A

To sort lines in descending order:

^KZ D

USAGE

To sort lines in a block of text, first mark the block and then press **^KZ**. The following prompt will appear on your screen:

Sort into ascending or descending order (A/D)?

Pressing **A** sorts in ascending order (A–Z) and pressing **D** sorts in descending order. The sorting starts with tabs, spaces, then numbers, then letters, and then symbols. (You can change this sequence with WSCHANGE). If you want to sort lines based on a column other than the leftmost column on the screen, switch to column block mode (by pressing **^KN**) and then mark the column on which you want the sort to be performed.

Speed Write

The following commands allow you to open a document without naming it first.

RELEASE

5 only

KEY SEQUENCE

S

or

File/Speed Write (new file)

USAGE

To open a document in WordStar without naming it first, use the Speed Write feature, either by pressing **S** from the Classic Opening menu or by selecting **File/Speed Write (new file)** from the pull-down Opening menu. The WordStar Edit screen will appear, but no file name will show on the left side of the status line. WordStar does not assign a default name to a Speed Write document. You must give it a name the first time you save it.

SEE ALSO

Document Mode
Nondocument Mode
Save

Spell

The following commands allow you to check the spelling in
your document.

RELEASE

4 and 5

KEY SEQUENCE

To check the spelling from the cursor position to the end of
your document:

^QL

or (in Release 5 only):

EDIT/Other/Check document spelling...

To check the spelling of a word at the current cursor location:

^QN

or (in Release 5 only):

EDIT/Other/Check word spelling...

To check the spelling of a word to be typed in:

^QO *<word>*

To check the spelling of the rest of the notes in a document (in Release 5 only):

^ONL

USAGE

To check the spelling of your document from the cursor position to the end, press **^QL** or select **Check document spelling...** from the EDIT/Other pull-down menu. If you want to check your whole document, press **^QR** or **^Home** first to reach the beginning of the document. When WordStar reaches a word it doesn't recognize (or, in Release 5, the same word twice in a row), the Spelling Check menu appears. The word appears in quotes followed by a numbered list of alternative spellings. Sometimes the entry

M display more suggestions

appears, indicating that there are more possible corrections than will fit on the screen. If the correct spelling is one of those shown in the numbered list, type the corresponding number and the new word will replace the old word in the text. If none of the words listed is correct, or if no suggestions for replacement are found, you have several options to choose from:

I   Ignores the word in rest of document

A   Adds word to personal dictionary

B   Bypasses word this time only

E   Lets you enter new word from keyboard

G   Turns global replacement on (or back off)

Release 4 only:

T   Turns auto-align off (or back on)

To check the spelling of a single word in your document, position the cursor anywhere within the word and press **^QN** or select **Check word spelling...** from the EDIT/Other pull-down menu. This command works like the ^QL command, except that some of the options are no longer relevant, such as **I** (ignore for rest of document).

To check the spelling of a word you have not yet entered into the text, press **^QO**. You will be prompted to enter a word to check. Options **G** and **B** are missing from the Spelling Check screen or dialog box for this command. If you have spelled the word correctly or found the right alternative, press **E** to enter the word into the text at the current cursor location.

To check the spelling of notes, press **^ONL**, which will check notes of all types for the rest of the document. To check all the notes in the document, press **^QC** or **^Home** first to make sure you initiate the procedure from the very beginning of the file.

Spreadsheet

The following commands allow you to insert data from a Lotus 1-2-3, Symphony, or Quattro spreadsheet into your WordStar document.

RELEASE

5 only

KEY SEQUENCE

^**KR** *<spreadsheet filename.ext >* *<cell range >*

or

EDIT/Edit/Insert a file...
<spreadsheet filename.ext > *<cell range >*

USAGE

To insert spreadsheet data from 1-2-3, Symphony, or Quattro as columns of text in WordStar, press ^**KR** or select **Insert a file...** from the EDIT/Edit pull-down menu, as if you were going to read a regular text block. Specify the spreadsheet name (such as **BUDGET.WK1**). WordStar automatically identifies which spreadsheet file format is being selected, based on the file's extension, and displays the cell range of the entire file onscreen. You can press ^**K** or **F10** to accept this cell range, or you can specify your own, using the column letter and row number of the first cell in the range, and then two periods (..) followed by the column letter and row number of the last cell in the range, just as you would when specifying the range in the spreadsheet program itself. Then press ^**K** or **F10**. The columns of data will be inserted into your WordStar text file at the cursor position. When performing this operation, remember that spreadsheets often have wide margins. Some adjustment may be necessary. For information on incorporating spreadsheets into merge print operations, see **Merge Print**.

SEE ALSO

Block Operations
Merge Print

Starting WordStar

The following commands allow you to start an installed copy of WordStar.

RELEASE

4 and 5

KEY SEQUENCE

To start WordStar and come to the Opening menu:

WS

To start WordStar and open a document file:

WS *<d:\pathname\filename.ext >*

To start WordStar and open a nondocument file in Release 4:

WS *<d:\pathname\filename.ext >* N

To start WordStar and open a nondocument file in Release 5:

WS *<d:\pathname\filename.ext >* /N

To start WordStar and print a specific file in Release 4:

WS *<d:\pathname\filename.ext >* P

To start WordStar and print a specific file in Release 5:

WS *<d:\pathname\filename.ext >* /P

To start WordStar, print a specific file, and then exit back to DOS in Release 4:

WS *<d:\pathname\filename.ext >* PX

To start WordStar, print a specific file, and then exit back to DOS in Release 5:

WS *<d:\pathname\filename.ext >* /P/X

USAGE

To start WordStar once it has been properly installed, type **WS** at the DOS prompt on the drive and directory where the WordStar program files reside. If you are using a hard disk system, you may want to specify this location using the DOS PATH command in a line in your AUTOEXEC.BAT file, as in the example below:

PATH C:\WORDSTAR;

where C is the hard disk drive letter and WORDSTAR is the directory where the WordStar program files are located. This command would make it possible to type **WS** from any directory on drive C to start WordStar. For more information on the DOS PATH command and the AUTOEXEC.BAT file, consult your DOS technical reference manual.

To start WordStar and open a specific file for editing, type **WS** and then the file name. If you are opening a nondocument file, type **N** after the file name in Release 4, or **/N** in Release 5. For all options following the file name you must precede the option with a slash (/) in Release 5. (In the rare case where you have configured WordStar so that nondocument mode is the default mode, you needn't type **N** or **/N** here; instead you must type **D** or **/D** after the file name if you want to open a document file.)

To start WordStar and print a specific file, type **WS** followed by the file name and then **P** or **/P**. To initiate the same procedure and exit WordStar on completion of printing, type **PX** instead of **P** or **/P/X** instead of **/P**.

SEE ALSO

Document Mode
Nondocument Mode
Print

Strike-Out

These commands turn strike-out printing on and off and
designate the strike-out character.

RELEASE

4 and 5

KEY SEQUENCE

To strike out text:

^PX<text >**^PX**

or (in Release 5 only):

EDIT/Style/Strikeout
<text >
EDIT/Style/Strikeout

To designate a strike-out character (in Release 5 only):

.XX A

where A is the new strike-out character.

USAGE

To strike out text (that is, print the text with a line through each character so that it appears stricken), press **^PX** or select **Strikeout** from the EDIT/Style pull-down menu where you want the strike-out to begin and press **^PX** or select **Strikeout** from the pull-down menu once more where you want it to end. This feature is used primarily in legal contexts where previously deleted clauses appear for reference in a contract. If you have control codes hidden, the text that you have struck out will appear brighter or in a different color. If you have control codes displayed, ^X markers will appear where you inserted the codes as well. To remove the strike-out, simply delete the codes. The character WordStar uses to strike out text is the dash or hyphen. You can change this character permanently in WSCHANGE or, in Release 5, you can change it temporarily by inserting the dot command **.XX** followed by the desired strike-out character.

Subscript and Superscript

These commands turn subscript and superscript printing on and off and designate the vertical position of the subscript and superscript text.

RELEASE

4 and 5

KEY SEQUENCE

To mark subscript text:

^PV *<text>* **^PV**

or (in Release 5 only):

EDIT/Style/Subscript
<text>
EDIT/Style/Subscript

To mark superscript text:

^PT *<text>* **^PT**

or (in Release 5 only):

EDIT/Style/Superscript
<text>
EDIT/Style/Superscript

To adjust the vertical position of sub- or superscript text:

.SR *n*

where *n* is the distance in 48ths of an inch that the marked text is lowered below the line (for subscript) or raised above the line (for superscript).

USAGE

To create subscript text, press **^PV** where you want the subscript to begin and **^PV** once more where you want it to end. To create superscript text, press **^PT** where you want the superscript to begin, and **^PT** once more where you want it to end. The vertical position will not change visibly on-screen except in Page Preview (**^OP**) in Release 5. If you have control codes hidden, the sub- or superscript text will appear brighter or in a different color. If you have control codes displayed, ^V markers will appear for subscript and ^T for superscript where you inserted the codes as well. To remove sub- or superscript, simply delete the codes. Depending on the capability of your printer, you can adjust the vertical position of sub- and superscript printing by inserting the dot command **.SR** followed by the desired vertical movement in 48ths of an inch. The default value is 3/48 in.

Synonyms

See **Thesaurus**.

Table of Contents

The following commands allow you to mark entries for tables of contents and other lists and to generate those lists.

RELEASE

4 and 5

KEY SEQUENCE

To mark an entry for a table of contents or one or more additional lists:

.TC [*n*] <*text* > **[#]**

or (in Release 5 only):

EDIT/Other/Table of contents entry.../ [*n*] <*text* > **[#]**

where *n* is the number (1–9) of the list.

To generate a table of contents and any other lists (from the Opening menu):

T <*file to which table of contents refers* >

USAGE

To create a table of contents, you must first create entries throughout the file using the dot command **.TC** followed by the table of contents entry, any spaces or dots (you can use the dot leader command (**^P.**) in Release 5 to insert rows of dots, called "dot leaders," between the entry and the page number), and then the pound sign (**#**) at the position on the line where you want page numbers, if any, to appear next to the entry. Insert these entries on a line above the headings to which they refer so that they will display the correct page number. If you want subheadings indented, add spaces or tabs after the **.TC** and before the text of the subentry.

To mark entries for additional lists, such as lists of illustrations or citations, follow the same procedure as above, but type a number (1–9) after **.TC** to indicate the number of the additional list. You can have up to ten lists in a single document.

Once all the entries for the table of contents and lists have been marked, press **T** or select **Other/Table of contents...** from the Opening menu to generate the table of contents and other lists. You will be prompted to specify a page range in case you don't want to include the whole file. Press ⏎ at these prompts to accept the default to use all pages.

WordStar then creates a new document for each list, with the same base file name as the file that contains the table of contents entries. The extension is **TOC** for the table of contents and **.TO1**, **.TO2**, and so on for the remaining lists. Once they are generated, you can edit these lists as regular document files.

SEE ALSO

Dot Leaders

Tabs

The following commands allow you to move to tab stops and set tab stops.

RELEASE

4 and 5

KEY SEQUENCE

The following table lists the commands enabling you to move
to and set tab stops:

COMMAND	FUNCTION
Tab *or* **^I**	Moves to next tab stop
^OI [#] *n**	Sets a tab stop (Release 4)
^OI [#] Esc	Sets a tab stop at current cursor position (Release 4)
^ON [#] *n**	Clears a tab stop (Release 4)
^ON [#] Esc	Clears a tab stop at the current cursor position (Release 4)
^ON A	Clears all tab stops (Release 4)
^OI<[#] *tab 1* [#] *tab* 2 [#] tab 3 *etc.*>**^K** [*or* **F10**] *or* EDIT/Layout/Margins and tabs... [select Tabs]<[#] *tab 1* [#] *tab 2 etc.*> **^K** [*or* **F10**] *or* **.TB**<[#] *tab 1* [#] *tab* 2 [#] *tab 3 etc.*>	Sets a tab stop (Release 5)
^OI ^T ^K [*or* **F10**] *or* EDIT/Layout/Margins and tabs... [select Tabs] **^T ^K** [*or* **F10**]	Clears all tab stops (Release 5)

*n is the column location of the tab stop

USAGE

Standard (left-aligning) tab stops are displayed on the ruler line as exclamation points (!) and decimal (period-aligning) tab stops are displayed as pound symbols (#). To move the cursor to the next tab stop on the ruler line, press **Tab** or **^I**. The cursor and any text to the right of it on that line will move to the right until it aligns with the next tab stop on the ruler line. If you are using the tab function to align columns with a proportionally spaced font, you may need to insert the fixed position character (**^P@**) at the tab stop before any text to make the columns align correctly; for more information see **Column Alignment**.

Standard tab stops arrange text so that it has a flush-left alignment. Decimal tab stops are used for numbers with decimal points (such as dollar amounts) and align columns at the decimal point. When you tab to a decimal tab stop, the word

Decimal

appears at the right side of the status line. As you type in a number (or other text), the characters move to the left of the tab stop until you type a period. After you do so, the characters move to the right of the decimal tab stop.

To set tab stops, press **^OI**. In Release 5, you can also either select **Margins and tabs...** from the EDIT/Layout pull-down menu or insert the dot command **.TB** followed by the tab stop settings.

If you have Release 4, after you have pressed **^OI** you will see a list of existing tab stops. The default stops are all regular tab stops at columns 6, 11, 16, 21, 26, 31, 36, 41, 46, 51, and 56. Specify a new tab stop by typing the column number, preceded by # if you want to specify a decimal tab stop. To create a new tab stop at the cursor position, press **^OI Esc**; if you want it to be a decimal tab stop, press **^OI # Esc** instead. You can set only one new tab stop at a time.

In Release 5 you have several ways to set tab stops. By pressing **^OI** or selecting **Margins and tabs...** from the EDIT/Layout pull-down menu, you access the MARGINS & TABS dialog box. **^OI** takes you to the tab stops option directly; if you use the pull-down menu you must then tab down to that option. You will see a list of the current tab stops each separated by a space. The default stops are all regular tab stops at .5", 1.0", 1.5", 2.0", 2.5", 3.0", 3.5", 4.0", 4.5", 5.0", and 5.5". Unlike Release 4, Release 5 allows you to set as many tab stops at this point as you want. For each tab stop you want to set, type in the column number or space in inches, or # followed by the column number or space in inches if you are setting a decimal tab stop. Separate each new tab stop setting with a space. When you enter your first number, the list of existing tab stops will disappear. If you just want to add some tab stops to the existing list, press ^R after you have added the new settings and the original list will reappear to the right of the new settings. You can also delete tab stops here by moving the cursor to a tab stop setting and deleting that number. When you are through adding and deleting tab stops, press ^K or F10 to accept the new settings. A line will appear in your document with the dot command .TB followed by the tab stops you designated.

You can also use the .TB command independently by typing the column numbers or space in inches for each tab stop, or # and column number or space in inches for each decimal tab stop, separated by a space.

To clear a tab stop in Release 4, press ^ON followed by the column number, or # and column number for a decimal tab stop. To clear all tab stops, press ^ON A. To clear a tab stop at the current cursor position, press ^ON Esc. To clear a decimal tab stop at the cursor position, press ^ON # Esc.

To clear all tab stops in Release 5, access the MARGINS & TABS dialog box in one of the ways described above, and then press ^Y followed by ^K or F10 to delete the tab stop entries in the dialog box entry field.

| SEE ALSO |

Column Alignment
Dot Leaders

Paragraph Margins
Proportional Spacing
Ruler Line

TelMerge

The following commands allow you to access the TelMerge
telecommunications program.

RELEASE

5 only

KEY SEQUENCE

From the Classic Opening menu:

AT

From the pull-down Opening menu:

Additional/ TelMerge

USAGE

To access the TelMerge program, type one of the key sequences listed above from the Opening menu. This program can
operate from within WordStar or by itself as a telecommunications program. A detailed description of this program
is outside the scope of this book. Please refer to the section on
TelMerge in your WordStar documentation.

Thesaurus

The following commands allow you to access the thesaurus feature, including word definitions (in Release 5).

RELEASE

4 and 5

KEY SEQUENCE

To load Word Finder at the DOS prompt (for Release 4 only):

D:\PATHNAME>WF

where D:\PATHNAME is the default drive and directory for Word Finder.

To access the Word Finder thesaurus in Release 4, position cursor on word to look up, then:

Alt-1

To access the thesaurus in Release 5, position cursor on word to look up, then:

^QJ

or

EDIT/Other/Thesaurus...

USAGE

In Release 4, the thesaurus program (called Word Finder) is a separate and independent program that must be loaded before you start WordStar. To do so, type **WF** at the DOS prompt, making sure you are in the drive and directory where the Word Finder files are stored. To access this thesaurus once you have started WordStar, press **Alt-1**. You can change the key combination that accesses Word Finder in the Word Finder installation program.

Once Word Finder is loaded and you are using WordStar, press **Alt-1** (or an alternative of your choosing) to find a list of synonyms and words of related meanings for the word on which the cursor is located. The Word Finder screen will appear, displaying the word you selected and below it a list of words of similar meaning, grouped by parts of speech (noun, verb, and so forth). The cursor will be on the first word in the list. To replace the word in your file with one from the list, use the cursor movement keys to select the word, and then press ↵. Sometimes the list of words is larger than the Word Finder screen. In this case, the message

MORE: PgDn

will appear at the top corner of the screen. You cannot use what is normally the equivalent WordStar control code, **^C**, to scroll to the next screen; you must press **PgDn**. To return to the first screen, press **PgUp**.

To look for synonyms for one of the words in the list, move the cursor to that word and press **Alt-1** (or your alternative) again. To exit without replacing your original word, press **Esc**.

If Word Finder cannot find the word you want to look up, it displays the message

The word was not found. Choose another one to look up.

along with a list of words closest to your selection in sound or spelling in the alphabetical listing of thesaurus entries. At this point, either move your cursor to an appropriate word or press **Esc** to abort the procedure.

In Release 5 the thesaurus has been incorporated into the main program; it is loaded when you start WordStar. To find words similar in meaning to a word in your document, position your cursor on the word you want to look up and either press **^QJ** or select **Thesaurus...** from the EDIT/Other pull-down menu. The word will appear in the top left corner of the Thesaurus menu in quotes, and the cursor will appear on the first word in the list of synonyms, which are grouped by parts of speech (noun, verb, and so forth). Sometimes the list of words is larger than the Thesaurus menu screen. Press **^C** or **PgDn** to find out if there are more synonyms. To return to a previous screen, press **^R** or **PgUp**.

At this point you have several options. To replace the word in your file with one from the list, select the word in the list using the cursor movement keys, and then press ↵. The word you looked up will be replaced by the alternative you selected. If you want to look up a new word instead at this point, press **I**. The SYNONYM LOOKUP dialog box appears. Enter the word you want to look up and press ↵. If you want to look up a word in the list, move your cursor to that word and press **L** for cross reference. To review the list for a previous word, press **P**. To look up the definition of a word, position the cursor on that word and press **K**. A brief definition will appear. Press **N** to see the next definition (if there is one) and **P** to see the previous one.

To leave the Thesaurus menu without making any changes, press **^U**. You cannot press **Esc** to exit here.

Time

The following commands allow you to insert the system time into your file.

RELEASE

4 and 5

KEY SEQUENCE ===========================

To insert the current system time as a text string in your document:

Esc-!

or (in Release 5 only):

Edit/Other/Shorthand macros .../!

To insert a code to print the current system time at time of merge printing:

&!&

USAGE =================================

In order for the time commands to function properly, you must set the DOS system time properly. (If your computer is equipped with an internal clock that sets the system time when you turn your computer on, this is not necessary.) To set the time, exit from WordStar. At the system prompt, type

C>TIME

Your system will display a message like:

Current time is 18:34:13.05
Enter new time:

If the time is correct, accept it by pressing ↵. If not, enter the correct time in the format shown, using the 24-hour (or military) format as shown above. (You can also set the time using the Run a DOS Command feature.)

To insert the time into the document, position your cursor at the place where you want the time to appear and press **Esc-!**. WordStar will insert the time in a simplified 12-hour format, which for the example above would be

6:34 PM

The time format can be changed using WSCHANGE. For more information, see Appendix A.

To print the current system time while merge printing, insert the code **&!&** at the place you want it to appear when printing. The time format will be the same as with **Esc-!**.

SEE ALSO

Date

Merge Print

Run a DOS Command

Time

Appendix A

Transfer Files between Releases

See **Print**.

Underline

These commands turn underlining on and off and designate whether to underline spaces between words.

RELEASE

4 and 5

KEY SEQUENCE

To underline text:

^PS *<text>* **^PS**

or

F3 *<text>* **F3**

or (in Release 5 only):

EDIT/Style/Underline
<text>
EDIT/Style/Underline

To turn the underlining of spaces on or off:

.UL ON/OFF

USAGE

To create underlined text, press **^PS** where you want the underlining to begin and **^PS** once more where you want it to end. On some monitors, underlining will be displayed on-screen; on others, it will appear brighter, dimmer, or in a different color. If you have control codes displayed, **^S** markers will appear where you inserted the codes as well. To remove underlining, simply delete the codes.

WordStar normally does not underline spaces that occur between underlining codes. To make it do so, insert the dot command **.UL ON**. To change it back to not underlining spaces, insert the dot command **.UL OFF**. You can change the default value using WSCHANGE (see Appendix A).

SEE ALSO

Appendix A

Undo

The following commands allow you to undo a command.

RELEASE

4 and 5

KEY SEQUENCE

^U *or* **F2**

or (in Release 5 only):

EDIT/Edit/Undo

| USAGE |

To undo a command, press ^U or **F2** or select **Undo** from the EDIT/Edit pull-down menu. You cannot undo every command in WordStar; undo is mainly used to "unerase," or recall the *last* section of text that has been deleted. When you are using one of the deletion commands, you will see a prompt telling you if the section of text is too large to unerase later and asking whether you are sure you want to delete it. The default amount of text WordStar can recall is 500 bytes or approximately 100 words; you can increase this up to 30,000 bytes using WSCHANGE. You cannot recall single character deletions.

WordStar also uses the undo command to cancel operations in submenus such as checking spelling or generating a table of contents. In Release 5, you must sometimes press **Esc** instead to abandon a menu command or exit a dialog box without performing the designated procedure.

The undo command does not undo cursor movement commands or remove text you have typed in.

| SEE ALSO |

Delete

Uppercase

See **Case Conversion.**

Variables

See **Merge Print.**

Window

The following commands allow you to manipulate screen windows. For block operations involving windows see **Block Operations**.

RELEASE

5 only

KEY SEQUENCE

To open or switch between windows:

^OK

or

EDIT/Window/Open/Switch between windows

To size the current window:

^OM *n*

or

EDIT/Window/Size current window.../*n*

where *n* is the number of lines the window is to occupy.

To close and save a window:

^KD *or* **F10**

or

EDIT/Window/Close and save window

To close and abandon changes to a window:

^KQ

or

EDIT/Window/Close and abandon window

USAGE

To open a second window, in effect splitting the Edit screen into two editing screens, press **^OK** or select **Open/Switch between windows** from the EDIT/Window pull-down menu. You will be asked to name the new window (since it is another document file). Name the new window and press ↵. A second ruler line will appear across the middle of the screen, with the cursor in the upper-left corner of the new (lower) window. The leftmost column of the status line will display the number 2 to indicate you are editing in the second window. To switch between windows, press **^OK** or select **Open/Switch between windows** again. The cursor moves to its most recent location in the first window, and the status line indicator now displays the number 1.

To make one of the windows vertically larger, press **^OM** or select **Open/Size current window...** from the EDIT/Window pull-down menu. The current window length will be displayed in lines. Enter a new value and press ↵. You are limited to the number of lines on your screen minus the status line and ruler lines; you cannot suppress ruler line display when you are using windows.

To close and save a window, either press **^KD** or **F10** or select **Close and save window** from the EDIT/Window pull-down menu. To close and abandon changes to a window, press **^KQ** or select **Close and abandon window** from the EDIT/Window pull-down menu.

SEE ALSO

Block Operations

Word Count

The following command allows you to determine the number of words in a file or marked block.

RELEASE

4 and 5

KEY SEQUENCE

To count the number of lines, words, and characters in a file or list of files in Release 4 from the DOS prompt:

WC *<filename1 filename2 filename3 >*

To count the number of words and characters in a marked block in Release 5:

^K?

USAGE

To count the words in a file or list of files with Release 4, you must use WC, an external utility program on the Program disk that is not loaded as part of WordStar. To use the word-count utility, type **WC** at the DOS prompt or use the Run a DOS Command feature (**^KF**) to access DOS, and then type **WC**, followed by the file name or names you want to count. The word count program will list the number of lines, words, and characters for each individual file as well as a grand total for all the files specified if there are more than one.

In Release 5, you can count the number of words and characters in a marked block from within WordStar. First mark the block and then press **^K?**. The number of words and characters in that block will be displayed.

SEE ALSO

Character Count

Run a DOS Command

Word Wrap

The following command allows you to turn word wrap off and on.

RELEASE

4 and 5

KEY SEQUENCE

^OW

USAGE

In document mode, WordStar normally inserts a soft return and moves text to the next line when it reaches the right margin; this feature is called word wrap. To suppress it, press **^OW**. When word wrap is suppressed, the text will continue to move to the right and your computer will beep as you pass the right margin. Turning off word wrap is primarily useful for working with tabular material that cannot wrap to the next line. To turn word wrap back on, press ^OW again.

| SEE ALSO |

Paragraph Alignment
Right Justification

APPENDIX A

Installing and Customizing WordStar

Release 4

The following is a brief description of the installation and customization procedures of WordStar Release 4. For information on making copies of your original program disks and other related topics, see the section entitled "Starting" in your WordStar documentation.

Installation

If you have a two-floppy disk system proceed as follows: after turning your computer on with the DOS system disk in drive A, take out the DOS system disk and place a copy of your Program disk in drive A and the Installation disk in drive B. Make sure you are logged onto drive B; your DOS prompt should look like this:

    B>

Next type **WINSTALL A:WS** ⏎ to reach the main menu of the Installation program.

    If you have a hard-disk system proceed as follows: after turning your computer on, make a directory on your hard disk drive called WS4 and log onto it. (You can give it another name, but you will need to change the program in several places if you do so. It is therefore best to use WS4.) To create this directory and log onto it, type

    MD WS4 ⏎
    CD WS4 ⏎

Your DOS prompt should look like this:

    C:\WS4>

(Your prompt may be simply **C>**.)

Next type **WINSTALL WS** ↵ to reach the Main Installation menu of the WINSTALL program.

From the Main Installation menu you can choose the more fundamental default settings for WordStar on your computer. Go through every option and change anything that does not reflect your preferences or your computer's configuration at this point. Don't be afraid if you make a mistake; anything you select here can be changed later.

First, select **A** (the Console menu) to choose your monitor type from the list provided, to select the method of displaying underlining, and to decide whether you want soft spaces (those inserted by WordStar for alignment as opposed to those you insert with the Spacebar). Press **X** when you are done with this menu to return to the Main Installation menu.

Next, select your default printer by pressing **B** (the Printer menu). You will see a list of printers and the currently installed printer (if you have never installed this copy of WordStar, it will show Draft Printer as the default). The list takes up four screens, so if your printer isn't on menu #1, press **2**, **3**, or **4** until you find it on the list. Select the printer you will be using most often; if you use more than one, you can select any other printer at print time by typing its name at the last prompt on the printing screen.

WordStar assumes that your printer is connected to the first parallel port (LPT1) on your printer. This is most often the correct setting, but if you are using a serial printer or your second parallel port, your printer will not respond. You must change the port setting in WSCHANGE. If your printer uses a sheet feeder, you must also specify this in WSCHANGE. See the **Customization** section below for more details. Press **X** when you are through with this menu to return to the Main Installation menu.

Next, select **C** for the Computer menu. From this menu, you designate the correct drive letters available on your computer, select the default drive for WordStar programs to reside (generally drive A for two-floppy systems and drive C for hard disk systems), select single-user or network use, and check the CONFIG.SYS file on your DOS system disk to make sure it is set correctly. (This file must contain the line **FILES=20** for WordStar to function properly.)

Finally, press **D** to access the Dictionaries menu and indicate which disk will contain your WordStar spelling dictionaries. Press **X** to return to the Main Installation menu and then **X** again to quit and save your changes; then press **Y** to affirm that choice.

At this point, WordStar has been installed to basically conform to the specifications of your computer system and your printer. For more refined adjustments, see **Customization** below.

Customization

WordStar allows for numerous customized settings, only some of which are applicable to every user. It is not within the scope of this book to describe every possible customized feature. What follows is a brief description of how WordStar's customization program, WSCHANGE, is structured in Release 4.

To load WSCHANGE with a two-floppy disk system, place your working copy of the WordStar program disk in drive A and the Installation disk in drive B. Log to drive B by pressing **B:** at the DOS prompt, and then type **WSCHANGE A:WS** ⏎. With a hard-disk system, assuming your WordStar program files are located on drive C in the directory WS4, type **CD C:\WS4** and then **WSCHANGE WS**.

The Main Installation menu will appear, looking much like the one in **WINSTALL**. From this menu you can select items in the following categories:

Console   Contains customization of such things as monitor selection and screen sizing, function key commands, video attributes (like screen colors, underlining, and reverse video).

Printer   Contains customization for all printer-related functions, such as setting the default printer, the printer port, the printer library, the size of the library of printers available, sheet feeder operation, and custom printer patches.

Computer   Contains customization of valid disk drive specifications, single-user or network setup, memory allocation, WordStar file names, directory search paths, and so on.

WordStar   Contains customization of page layout settings, editing defaults, help level settings, spelling checks, indexing, merge printing, shorthand macros, and nondocument mode.

Patching   Contains advanced customization access to WordStar program code for experienced programmer-level customization.

Release 5

The following is a brief description of the installation and customization procedures of WordStar Release 5. For information on making copies of your original program disks and other related topics, see the section entitled "Starting" in your WordStar documentation.

Installation

If you have a two-floppy disk system proceed as follows: after turning your computer on with the DOS system disk in drive A, take out the DOS system disk and place a copy of your Program disk in drive A and the Installation disk in drive B. Make sure you are logged onto drive B; your DOS prompt should look like this:

B>

Next type **WINSTALL A:WS** ↵ to reach the main menu of the Installation program.

If you have a hard-disk system proceed as follows: after turning your computer on, make a directory on your hard disk drive called WS5 and log onto it. (You can give it another name, but you will need to change the program in several places if you do so. It is therefore best to use WS5.) To create this directory and log onto it, type

```
MD  WS5  ↵
CD  WS5  ↵
```

Your DOS prompt should look like this:

```
C:\WS5>
```

(Your prompt may only appear as **C>**.) Next type **WINSTALL WS** ↵ to reach the Main Installation menu of the WINSTALL program.

From the Main Installation menu you can choose the more fundamental default settings for WordStar on your computer. Go through every option and change anything that does not reflect your preferences or your computer's configuration at this point. Don't be afraid if you make a mistake; anything you select here can be changed later.

First, select **A** (the Console menu) to choose your monitor type from the list provided, to select the method of displaying underlining, to decide whether you want soft spaces (those inserted by WordStar for alignment as opposed to those you insert with the Spacebar), and to select monochrome or color default settings. Press **X** when you are done with this menu to return to the Main Installation menu.

Next, select your default printer by pressing **B** (the Printer menu). You will see a list of printers and the currently installed printer (if you have never installed this copy of WordStar, it will use Draft Printer as the default). The list takes up several screens, so if your printer isn't on the first one, press **PgDn** until it appears on the screen. If you intend to use more than one printer, you will need to select them one at a time. After you select a printer to install, a printer driver file (with the file extension **.PDF**) will be created for each printer you install. You will be prompted to name the file (using the first eight letters of a DOS file name).

You will next see an Additional Installation menu. At this point, add or remove any resident fonts before selecting that option. Next, WordStar assumes that your printer is connected to the first parallel port (LPT1) on your computer. This is most often the correct setting, but if you are using a serial printer or your second parallel port, your printer will not respond. You must change the port setting now if LPT1 is not correct. If your printer uses a sheet feeder, you should also specify this now on the Additional Installation menu. You can view, save to a file, or print specific notes concerning your printer at this point as well. Press Esc twice when you are through with this menu to return to the Main Installation menu.

Next, press **C** to select your default printer (the printer that WordStar assumes you are using when no other printer is specified at print time). Select the letter next to the printer of your choice from the menu, and then press **X** to return to the Main Installation Menu.

Press **D** to access the Computer menu. From this menu, you designate the correct drive letters available on your computer, select the default drive for WordStar programs to reside (generally drive A for two-floppy systems and drive C for hard disk systems), select single-user or network use, and check the CONFIG.SYS and AUTOEXEC.BAT files on your DOS system disk to make sure they are set up correctly. CONFIG.SYS must contain the line **FILES=20** for WordStar to function properly.

Next, press **E** to access the Dictionaries menu and indicate which disk will contain your WordStar spelling dictionaries. Press **X** to return to the Main Installation menu.

Finally, press **F** to select the menu system you would prefer: the WordStar Classic menu system or the new pull-down menu system. Then press **X** twice again to quit and save your changes, and press **Y** to affirm that choice.

At this point, WordStar has been installed to basically conform to the specifications of your computer system and your printer. If you made changes to your system's CONFIG.SYS or AUTOEXEC.BAT files, press the **Ctrl**, **Alt**, and **Del** keys simultaneously to reboot your computer and load the changes into memory. For more refined adjustments, see **Customization** below.

Customization

WordStar allows for numerous customized settings, only some of which are applicable to every user. It is not within the scope of this book to describe every possible customized feature. What follows is a brief description of how WordStar's customization programs, WSCHANGE and PRCHANGE, are structured in Release 5.

WSCHANGE

To load WSCHANGE with a two-floppy disk system, place your working copy of the WordStar program disk in drive A and the Installation disk in drive B. Log to drive B by pressing **B:** at the DOS prompt and then type **WSCHANGE A:WS** ↵. With a hard-disk system, assuming your WordStar program files are located on drive C in the directory WS5, type **CD C:\WS5** and then **WSCHANGE WS**.

The Main Installation menu will appear, looking much like the one in **WINSTALL**. From this menu you can select items in the following categories:

Console   Contains customization of such things as monitor selection and screen sizing, function key commands, video attributes (like screen colors, underlining, and reverse video).

Printer   Contains customization for all printer-related functions, such as choosing a printer, setting the default printer, the printer port, sheet feeder operation, and custom printer patches.

Computer   Contains customization of valid disk drive specifications, single-user or network setup, memory allocation, WordStar file names, directory search paths and so on.

WordStar   Contains customization of page layout set-
            tings, editing defaults, help level settings,
            spelling checks, indexing, merge printing,
            shorthand macros, and nondocument mode.

Patching   Contains advanced customization access to
            WordStar program code for experienced
            programmer-level customization.

PRCHANGE

PRCHANGE is a new program utility that allows you to install new printers and modify your PDF files (for example, to
install new fonts or cartridges) without going through the entire process of installation. To load PRCHANGE with a two-
floppy disk system, place your working copy of the WordStar
program disk in drive A and the Installation disk in drive B.
Log to drive B by pressing **B:** at the DOS prompt and then
type **PRCHANGE A:WS** ↵. With a hard-disk system, assuming your WordStar program files are located on drive C in the
directory WS5, type **C:\WS5** and then **PRCHANGE WS**.

There are three options on the Main Menu: Install a printer,
Modify PDF settings, and Quit and save changes. You can
also abandon the PRCHANGE operation without saving any
changes by pressing **Esc** from the Main Menu.

If you are adding a printer (or a printer configuration, such
as a Hewlett-Packard LaserJet Series II with the B font
cartridge and manual feed), select **Install a printer**. If you are
making changes to an existing print driver file, select **Modify
PDF settings**. You should use this option when you want to
add new soft fonts or cartridges to your printer configuration.
When you are through making changes, select **Quit and save
changes** from the Main menu to exit.

Selections from The SYBEX Library

WORD PROCESSING

The ABC's of WordPerfect (Second Edition)
Alan R. Neibauer
300pp. Ref. 504-2
This introduction explains the basics of desktop publishing with WordPerfect 5: editing, layout, formatting, printing, sorting, merging, and more. Readers are shown how to use WordPerfect 5's new features to produce great-looking reports.

The ABC's of WordPerfect
Alan R. Neibauer
239pp. Ref. 425-9
This basic introduction to WordPefect consists of short, step-by-step lessons— for new users who want to get going fast. Topics range from simple editing and formatting, to merging, sorting, macros, and more. Includes version 4.2

Mastering WordPerfect 5
Susan Baake Kelly
475pp. Ref. 500-X
The revised and expanded version of this definitive guide is now on WordPerfect 5 and covers wordprocessing and basic desktop publishing. As more than 100,000 readers of the original edition can attest, no tutorial approaches it for clarity and depth of treatment. Sorting, line drawing, and laser printing included.

Mastering WordPerfect
Susan Baake Kelly
435pp. Ref. 332-5
Step-by-step training from startup to mastery, featuring practical uses (form letters, newsletters and more), plus advanced topics such as document security and macro creation, sorting and columnar math. Includes Version 4.2.

Advanced Techniques in WordPerfect 5
Kay Yarborough Nelson
500pp. Ref. 511-5
Now updated for Version 5, this invaluable guide to the advanced features of WordPerfect provides step-by-step instructions and practical examples covering those specialized techniques which have most perplexed users – indexing, outlining, foreign-language typing, mathematical functions, and more.

Advanced Techniques in WordPerfect
Kay Yarborough Nelson
400pp. Ref. 431-3
Exact details are presented on how to accomplish complex tasks including special sorts, layered indexing, and statistical typing. Includes details on laser printing operations.

WordPerfect Desktop Companion
SYBEX Ready Reference Series
Greg Harvey/Kay Yarbourough Nelson
663pp. Ref. 507-7

This compact encyclopedia offers detailed, cross-referenced entries on every software feature, organized for fast, convenient on-the-job help. Includes self-contained enrichment material with tips, techniques and macros. Special information is included about laser printing using WordPerfect that is not available elsewhere. For Version 4.2.

WordPerfect 5 Desktop Companion
SYBEX Ready Reference Series
Greg Harvey/Kay Yarborough Nelson
700pp. Ref. 522-0

Desktop publishing features have been added to this compact encyclopedia. This title offers more detailed, cross-referenced entries on every software features including page formatting and layout, laser printing and word processing macros. New users of WordPerfect, and those new to Version 5 and desktop publishing will find this easy to use for on-the-job help. For Version 5.

WordPerfect Tips and Tricks (Second Edition)
Alan R. Neibauer
488pp. Ref. 489-5

This new edition is a real timesaver. For on-the-job guidance and creative new uses for WordPerfect, this title covers all new features of Version 4.2 – including tables of authorities, concordance files, new print enhancements and more.

WordPerfect Instant Reference
SYBEX Prompter Series
Greg Harvey/Kay Yarborough Nelson
254pp. Ref. 476-3

When you don't have time to go digging through the manuals, this fingertip guide offers clear, concise answers: command summaries, correct usage, and exact keystroke sequences for on-the-job tasks. Convenient organization reflects the structure of WordPerfect.

Mastering SAMNA
Ann McFarland Draper
503pp. Ref. 376-7

Word-processing professionals learn not just how, but also when and why to use SAMNA's many powerful features. Master the basics, gain power-user skills, return again and again for reference and expert tips.

The ABC's of MicroSoft WORD
Alan R. Neibauer
250pp. Ref. 497-6

Users who want to wordprocess straightforward documents and print elegant reports without wading through reams of documentation will find all they need to know about MicroSoft WORD in this basic guide. Simple editing, formatting, merging, sorting, macros and style sheets are detailed.

Mastering Microsoft WORD (Second Edition)
Matthew Holtz
479pp. Ref. 410-0

This comprehensive, step-by-step guide includes Version 3.1. Hands-on tutorials treat everything from word processing basics to the fundamentals of desktop publishing, stressing business applications throughout.

Advanced Techinques in Microsoft WORD
Alan R. Neibauer
537pp. Ref. 416-X

The book starts with a brief overview, but the main focus is on practical applications using advanced features. Topics include customization, forms, style sheets, columns, tables, financial documents, graphics and data management.

Mastering DisplayWrite 3
Michael E. McCarthy
447pp. Ref. 340-6

Total training, reference and support for users at all levels – in plain, non-technical language. Novices will be up and running in an hour's time; everyone will gain complete word-processing and document-management skills.

Mastering MultiMate Advantage II
Charles Ackerman
407pp. Ref. 482-8

This comprehensive tutorial covers all the capabilities of MultiMate, and highlights the differences between MultiMate Advantage II and previous versions – in pathway support, sorting, math, DOS access, using dBASE III, and more. With many practical examples, and a chapter on the On-File database.

Mastering MultiMate Advantage
Charles Ackerman
349pp. Ref. 380-5

Master much more than simple word processing by making the most of your software. Sample applications include creating expense reports, maintaining customer lists, merge-printing complex documents and more.

The Complete Guide to MultiMate
Carol Holcomb Dreger
208pp. Ref. 229-9

This step-by-step tutorial is also an excellent reference guide to MultiMate features and uses. Topics include search/replace, library and merge functions, repagination, document defaults and more.

Advanced Techniques in MultiMate
Chris Gilbert
275pp. Ref. 412-7

A textbook on efficient use of MultiMate for business applications, in a series of self-contained lessons on such topics as multiple columns, high-speed merging, mailing-list printing and Key Procedures.

The ABC's of WordStar Release 5
Alan Simpson
300pp. Ref. 516-6

This quick guide to getting started on WordStar Release 5's full capabilities covers editing, formatting, printing good-looking documents and more detailed word processing tasks. Ideal for the new user who wants an uncomplicated introduction.

Mastering WordStar Release 5
Greg Harvey
425pp. Ref. 491-7

Harvey's complete tutorial and reference guide covers all the features of WordStar Release 5 from elementary to advanced, and highlights functions new to this release. Better document processing, editing, and printing are emphasized throughout with examples.

Mastering WordStar Release 4
Greg Harvey
413pp. Ref. 399-6

Practical training and reference for the latest WordStar release – from startup to advanced featues. Experienced users will find new features highlighted and illustrated with hands-on examples. Covers math, macros, laser printers and more.

Introduction to WordStar 2000
David Kolodney/Thomas Blackadar
292pp. Ref. 270-1

This engaging, fast-paced series of tutorials covers everything from moving the cursor to print enhancements, format files, key glossaries, windows and MailMerge. With practical examples, and notes for former WordStar users.

Introduction to WordStar (Second Edition)
Arthur Naiman
208pp. Ref. 134-9
This all time bestseller is an engaging first-time introduction to word processing as well as a complete guide to using Word-Star – from basic editing to blocks, global searches, formatting, dot commands, SpellStar and MailMerge.

Practical Techniques in WordStar Release 5
Julie Anne Arca
350pp. Ref. 495-X
Arca's classic is fully revised to cover WordStar 5's latest features. Designed to lead readers through step-by-step examples and exercises, this user-friendly title has sold over 100,000 copies in the original edition.

Mastering Wordstar on the IBM PC (Second Edition)
Arthur Naiman
200pp. Ref. 392-9
A specially revised and expanded introduction to Wordstar with SpellStar and MailMerge. Reviewers call it "clearly written, conveniently organized, generously illustrated and definitely designed from the user's point of view."

Practical WordStar Uses
Julie Anne Arca
303pp. Ref. 107-1

A hands-on guide to WordStar and MailMerge applications, with solutions to comon problems and "recipes" for day-to-day tasks. Formatting, merge-printing and much more; plus a quick-reference command chart and notes on CP/M and PC-DOS.

Practical Techniques in WordStar Release 4
Julie Anne Arca
334pp. Ref. 465-8
A task oriented approach to WordStar Release 4 and the DOS operating system. Special applications are covered in detail with summaries of important commands and step-by-step instructions.

WordStar Tips and Traps
Dick Andersen/Cynthia Cooper/Janet McBeen
239pp. Ref. 261-2
A real time-saver. Hundreds of self-contained entries, arranged by topic, cover everything from customization to dealing with the DISK FULL error to key-stroke programming. Includes MailMerge and CorrectStar.

Advanced Techniques in WordStar 2000
John Donovan
350pp. Ref. 418-6
This task-oriented guide to Release 2 builds advanced skills by developing practical applications. Tutorials cover everything from simple printing to macro creation and complex merging. With MailList, StarIndex and TelMerge.

SYBEX Computer Books
are different.

Here is why . . .

At SYBEX, each book is designed with you in mind. Every manuscript is carefully selected and supervised by our editors, who are themselves computer experts. We publish the best authors, whose technical expertise is matched by an ability to write clearly and to communicate effectively. Programs are thoroughly tested for accuracy by our technical staff. Our computerized production department goes to great lengths to make sure that each book is well-designed.

In the pursuit of timeliness, SYBEX has achieved many publishing firsts. SYBEX was among the first to integrate personal computers used by authors and staff into the publishing process. SYBEX was the first to publish books on the CP/M operating system, microprocessor interfacing techniques, word processing, and many more topics.

Expertise in computers and dedication to the highest quality product have made SYBEX a world leader in computer book publishing. Translated into fourteen languages, SYBEX books have helped millions of people around the world to get the most from their computers. We hope we have helped you, too.

For a complete catalog of our publications:

SYBEX, Inc. 2021 Challenger Drive, #100, Alameda, CA 94501
Tel: (415) 523-8233/(800) 227-2346   Telex: 336311
Fax: (415) 523-2373